The New Face of Aging

Also by Mike Magee, M.D.:

    The Best Medicine

    Positive Doctors in America

    Positive Leadership

    The Pfizer Medical School Manual

Also by Michael D'Antonio:

    The Best Medicine

    Atomic Harvest

    Heaven on Earth

    Fall From Grace

The New Face of Aging

Stories from Senior Olympians

Mike Magee, M.D.
and
Michael D'Antonio

Spencer Books, New York

SPENCER BOOKS

Book design by Bob Williamson

Library of Congress Cataloging-in-Publication Data

Magee, Mike, M.D.
The new face of aging: stories from senior olympians
/ Mike Magee and Michael D'Antonio.—1st ed.
184 p.   22 x 15 cm
ISBN 1-889793-08-6
1. Healthy Aging.   2. Senior athletes case studies.
I. D'Antonio, Michael   II. Title   R727.3 M34   2001
610.69" – DC21   01-15937

First Edition: January, 2001
Printed in Canada

Dedication

James Ward
1917-2000

*In memory of Jim Ward who died while riding his
bike before this book was published.*

*Mr. Ward's 83 years of enthusiastic living are an
inspiration and an example of the values and spirit
of all the seniors who share their stories here.*

Contents

Acknowledgments

We thank the individual athletes and their families for sharing their stories and their lives with us.

This book would not have been possible without the help of Dilia Santana who skillfully guided the process and its many steps to completion. Thanks as well to Eneida Clarke and Joanne Blakely for their supporting roles.

Finally, we offer our gratitude to our families for their support and patience throughout this project.

Introduction

The New Era

We have entered the new era of longevity. Once mainly the domain of fiction, life extension — through science, lifestyle, and technology — has become a reality. And you are already enjoying the benefits of these developments, whether you realize it or not. If you have any doubt, consider some of these facts:

• In the past century average American life expectancies have risen from 49 years to 76.

• In our time the historic record for longevity was set by Frenchwoman, Jean Calment, who in 1997 died in her 123rd year.

• The number of very old Americans has increased dramatically. The Census Bureau estimates that today more than 66,000 have reached age 100. This is almost double the number in 1990, and fifteen times the number of centenarians counted in 1950.

• Life at age 100 is remarkably healthy. As a group, centenarians suffer fewer health problems than those ten or fifteen years younger. The death rate for this age group is lower, too, than it is among people between 75 and 85.

The numbers do not lie. The human lifespan is stretching forward, promising us all the chance to live many years longer than previous generations. On its own this is good news. But once we understand the potential for a longer life, we immediately begin to wonder about the quality of these extra years. For generations old age has suffered from a rather dismal image. Many picture it as a time of infirmity and dependence. But here again, the facts of a longer life are very encouraging:

• "Old Age" does not mean illness. A recent MacArthur Foundation study found that a substantial majority of 80-year olds reported they suffered from no disabilities. And even after age 85, almost half said they were fully functional. According to the National Council on Aging, 86 percent of people over age 65 report no significant health problems.

• Dependence is not the norm, even for the very old. Poverty is no higher among senior citizens than it is in the general population. Only one out of twenty people older than 65 live in nursing homes, and that number is declining. Among centenarians, one in six still lived alone.

• The loss of mental acuity, long associated with aging, is not inevitable. Scientific experiments have found that with "brain exercise" the loss of cognitive functioning and memory associated with age are greatly reduced. Studies of centenarians found that up until age 95, the majority suffered no serious cognitive problems.

• "Middle Age" is stretching. One-third of the 70-year olds recently surveyed by the Harris organization included themselves in the definition of "mid life." A full 44 percent described their mature years as the best time in their lives. This is compared with 32 percent who said the same thing in 1974.

Science and Aging

As impressive as all these facts may be, they pale in comparison to what science tells us about the potential for living longer and living healthier. Medicine has made astounding leaps forward in the past one hundred years, eliminating many of the causes of death that plagued previous generations. Treatments for cancer, heart disease, and other ailments are being improved continually; and research on other life-robbing illnesses is promising indeed. Science is even beginning to unlock the puzzle of Alzheimers, long perhaps the most dreaded illness associated with aging.

All of medical science is likely to take a quantum leap forward based on the rapid progress of several groups now analyzing the human genome. Gene science will aid longevity in two ways. First, it will provide screening and treatments for illness. (Gene therapies for cancer and other life-threatening illnesses are envisioned.) Second, it will isolate what some researchers call "supergenes" responsible for the extraordinary good health and longevity enjoyed by a distinct group of high-functioning, older people. It is quite possible that gene products can be developed to provide us with the benefits of these good genes even if we are not born with them. This has already been done with some tiny organisms, which have had their lifespans doubled through genetic manipulations.

Lifestyle and Aging

While science promises much for tomorrow, today we live with the genes we have been given by nature. With average genes, experts say we all have the potential to reach age 85, at least. Understanding this, we must all then wonder why some people manage to reach such an old age in relative health and others do not. The answer, we suspect, lies in lifestyle — the "nurture" side of the age-old nature/ nurture equation.

Studies of the health habits of the very old are not yet conclusive. When Harvard Medical School studied 169 people aged 100 and more, they showed no consistent pattern in diet and exercise. The fact that these extremely old people did not follow one pathway suggests that when it comes to reaching 100, genes may be vitally important. But studies do point to many factors that can make life in the sixties, seventies, and eighties better for the more ordinarily old. Among them are:

• Regular exercise is good. There is no controversy over the benefits of even moderate exercise — 20 minutes every other day. The risk of heart disease, high blood pressure, and diabetes are all reduced by exercise. Many studies have also suggested exercise will reduce your chance of stroke and some cancers. In addition to aerobic exercise, weight training is recommended to maintain muscle and mobility.

• Medical check-ups that can detect certain illnesses, especially cancer, do increase our chances of living longer and healthier.

• A moderate diet is beneficial. Obesity is linked with diabetes, heart disease, and some kinds of cancer. Low-fat, high-fiber diets are believed to be most beneficial. And some supplements, including low-dose aspirin tablets and anti-oxidant vitamins are also linked to better health. Both men and women benefit from calcium to prevent osteoporosis.

The Flavor of Aging

The studies and surveys that have yielded general information about health and longevity are consistent when it comes to the facts of older peoples' lives, but they do not capture much of the flavor. After all, the essence of life is not just how we function, but how we feel. The revolution in aging that is now underway is not just a biological phenomenon but a social and spiritual one as well.

In partnership with Pfizer Inc, the National Senior Games Association recently surveyed participants in Senior Olympics events to discover their attitudes and experiences. As athletes, they are more active than the typical senior is and, in fact, more active than many people of a much younger age. Most of the senior athletes said they played for the love of the game, not just to win. They enjoyed the activity, devoting between three to seven hours per week to practice.

The fact that these athletes play for the love of the game is not especially surprising. Indeed, they all seemed to share a youthful enthusiasm for play — simply for the sake of enjoyment — as a vital aspect of a well-rounded life. What is surprising is how many of these more active, healthy elder Americans mentioned the same three social keys — we came to call them "The Three Cs" — as keys to their wellbeing.

The "3-Cs" of Aging

The first "C" is Staying Current. More than two thirds of the most active seniors are regular users of the Internet. This is compared with just 14 percent in their peer groups. In our interviews most of the 24 seniors who told their stories said they use the Internet to communicate vie e-mail and to do research on topics of interest. Fifty-five percent use the World Wide Web to research health topics. The seniors in our study also said they were avid readers of books and periodicals.

The second "C" is Staying Connected. Relationships with mates, children, extended family, and friends were often mentioned as core values. Indeed, surveys have found that loneliness is more of a problem among the young than the old. More than 40 percent of the seniors we surveyed held paying jobs, maintaining their connection to the community and the workplace. They said they value relationships far more than possessions and many mentioned the social interaction with other athletes as the main draw of the Senior Games.

The third "C" is Staying in Control. Though 64 percent of the seniors had chronic diseases requiring medication, they reported they control their illness and the illness did not control them. The nursing-home model of old age fits fewer people every year. Modern medicine is extending the period when people can live independently. At the same time the vast majority of seniors do have the financial resources to maintain independent households.

Today's Face of Aging

As "the new face of aging" becomes clearer to see, the public view of growing older is changing too. Where the retiring senior was once viewed as crabby, dependent, lonely, and costly, maturing seniors are now described as independent, friendly, busy, and productive. Seniors are highly functional, engaged, and productive role models who can also serve as wise critics and guides. The question for younger members of society is no longer whether mature seniors can keep up with us, but rather, can we keep up with them.

Though the 24 athletes profiled in this book are each extraordinary in their own ways, role models for a vital old age can be found in every community in America. Their examples are rubbing off on the rest of us, making the entire country more optimistic about aging. In 1974 more than half of Americans said that chronic poor health is a hallmark of old age. Many public-policy experts looked at the baby-boom generation and began to fear a future "pandemic" of old age and disability. In the year 2000 less than 40 percent of the general public believe this will happen. More remarkably, 84 percent would be happy to live to age 90.

Tomorrow's Face of Aging

The 24 athletes portrayed in this book offer a glimpse of how life can be as we approach age 90 and beyond. Their lives suggest that healthy, productive years can march on and on after the traditional retirement age of 65. In all cases they stress preserving and maximizing health. Longevity is a side benefit. Through their examples they suggest the habits and attitudes we might all embrace. And they offer the most valuable and precious element of a life well lived: *hope for the future.*

I

Ordinary Heroes

In the world of senior athletes live millions of men and women who quietly pursue a passion in sports. On the outside, they may seem like everyday people. But on the inside, they burn with a competitive spirit and a joy of accomplishment that fill their entire lives with an optimistic glow.

ELEANOR SCOTT

Vaccinated Against Depression

Eleanor Scott is a very physical person. One minute she's just standing and talking in the cluttered kitchen of her 100-year-old farmhouse. The next, she's thrown herself on the floor to demonstrate the worm-like wriggling she had to perform while spelunking recently in a Colorado cave with people half her age. She then jumps up and throws one leg on the counter so she can stretch out her hamstring.

At 70 years of age, Scott is a short, muscular woman with blue eyes, white hair, and the smallest of potbellies caused, she says, "by a Danish diet of too much butter and bacon." She is remarkably fit even for a senior athlete. "I really don't ever get tired when I'm competing," she explains. "Something about being involved in the Senior Games just energizes me."

Indeed, Scott's life practically revolves around the games. An administrator for her local and regional competitions, she has turned a former sunroom in her house into an office with computer equipment and stacks of literature and sign-up sheets. Her phone rings constantly with calls from organizers, volunteers, and contestants. The answering machine announces that callers have reached her home AND the local Senior Games' office.

"Sometimes it seems like this is my life," she says with a smile. "It makes me feel like even though I'm getting older, I am not letting go of my life."

*   *   *

Life wasn't always so bright for Eleanor Scott. Twenty-five years ago she was a college physical-education instructor who was raising four children, coaching a gymnastics team, and feeling worn out. "I remember turning 45 and then 46 and thinking, My God, I'm now old."

She had reason to feel tired. At age 39 Scott had discovered a lump in her breast and was diagnosed with cancer. The year was 1969 and the options for treatment were few. Doctors recommended a radical mastectomy and she underwent the operation, which included removing several important muscles.

"It can be a devastating thing," says Scott. "I mean, I joined a support group and there was one lady in it who was much younger than me and simply said, 'I'm never going to leave my house.' And you know, I don't think she did."

Scott was not so distraught that she hid herself away, but she did suffer both physically and psychologically. Then, at about the time when she was deciding that she was old and tired, some colleagues at work took up running. They were roughly her age, but in a short time seemed to develop real strength and stamina.

"They were pretty funny," she recalls. "They would run up to me and then do circles around me saying, 'Look what we can do.'" The good-natured taunts were enough to get Scott to begin running herself. Soon she was feeling stronger and younger. Ten years would pass before she saw a poster for the New York State Senior Games, which were being held at a state college in Cortland. She realized that at 56 she was old enough to compete and, on a lark, drove there alone.

"It lasted four days and I had a wonderful time," she recalls. "I did discus, shot-put, javelin, high jump, 100 meters, long jump and swimming. The thing was, I felt a strong desire to do my best. Before each event I felt sort of nervous and anxious and excited. But I also felt like I could do it. And each time, I did. It's a real confidence booster." When she went home, she began training for the next competition, setting up hurdles in her yard and running along the local streets.

*   *   *

Many senior athletes report that the confidence they gain as they develop skills and engage in competition is reminiscent of the spirit they felt at play when they were much younger. As a child growing up in Flatbush, Brooklyn, Scott was a dedicated athlete and a bit of a tomboy. She felt capable and competent, and today she feels the same way.

"I like to do everything like I mean it," says Scott. "I even have a very strong, assertive signature. It's not all shaky, the way some people's are. I'm getting older, but I'm not letting go of life."

*   *   *

Recently Scott took on a new sport, pole vaulting, when it became available at the state games. She had to learn it on the spot. "They taught me how to hold the pole and how to run. I just did it and I got over the bar." Just getting over the bar proved to be enough to win a gold medal and defeat her chief rival, a woman from a neighboring town. "Her name is Rosalia and she really is my nemesis," laughs Scott. "The competition is friendly but believe me, it's real."

Scott believes deeply in the power of play and adventure, whether she's exploring caves, climbing rocks, or throwing the discus. "Put me in the woods anywhere, preferably with a tent, and I'll be just fine," she says with a smile. These activities and her involvement with other athletes and the organization of local games offer her friendship, health, competition, and a chance to use her talents.

"It doesn't make life all roses," concedes Scott. Indeed, she copes with many of the challenges that parents face in later life, including responsibility for her retired Army-officer son who is disabled, and caring for an infant grandchild. "I do believe in God!" she says. "After all, if you don't have that, you have no invisible means of support." And she keeps very active.

"There is so much to look forward to. Every time I get into a new age group there are new people to compete with and new records to go after. If you ask me, it's a vaccine against depression and I take it all the time."

ARTHUR AND JACKIE MURPHY

Where Did the Day Go?

It is fitting that Jackie and Arthur Murphy met at a roller rink that was roughly half way between their childhood homes on Long Island.

The year was 1954. He was 22 years old and she was 18. They both loved to skate, and in fact they both loved and played all sports from stickball to basketball. Soon they would love each other. They were married within the year, and have been together ever since, spinning like skaters, through three children, two grandchildren and now, retirement.

At a moment in life when many couples choose to slow down, the Murphys may be more active than ever. They both participate at local, state, and national Senior Games. They have each won a fistful of medals. Their big sport is shuffleboard, but Arthur also plays pocket billiards when it is offered. The competition is exciting for both, but Jackie admits her desire to win burns hotter.

"I am competitive to a fault," says Jackie, who is a short, curly-haired woman with an athletic body. She has arthritis and carpal tunnel syndrome, but finds the activity helps her feel better. "I may even want to win too much," she admits. "It gives me butterflies beforehand, and when I lose I do feel a little down."

In a bit of a role reversal, at least when it comes to sexist clichés, Arthur says he finds the relationships he forms in sport, and the process of helping others learn and improve, far more rewarding than a victory on the court or pool table. One of his most pleasant memories of competition was a long day spent at the pool tables during the Empire State Senior Games. He remembers clearly the spirited play of the most senior competitor, who was 85 years old and had little trouble keeping up with much younger men.

"We have made friends that have stayed friends for a long time. We correspond with them on the Internet and we meet them at the national and state games. It's really great to make new friends at any age."

These friends stay in touch via e-mail and regular letters. Sometimes they send surprise gifts. After a trip to one out-of-state competition, Artie sent a note of thanks and a macrame holder for potted plants he had made himself to a gal in Tucson, Arizona. As a thank you to him, she then sent him a box containing a beautiful hand-thrown pot.

*   *   *

Arthur and Jackie Murphy count the friends and the experiences they have had in senior athletic competition among the most important things in their life together. They only took up shuffleboard as seniors, and have discovered in the game a remarkably competitive sport subculture.

"Oh, there are people who take it very seriously, and there are certain states — like Florida — where the game is played at a very high level," explains Jackie. "I mean, we are lucky here in New York if we can find a court to play on that isn't all cracked and slanted. In Florida they have big clubs with perfect courts where they lay glass beads down for the disk to float on. People play seven days a week. The strategy is very sophisticated, and the players have a lot of skill."

The Murphys remember with both fondness and chagrin one of their recent encounters with elite players from a club in Florida. "We were at the nationals," recalls Arthur. "These two men, one of them a preacher, were such superior players that they could have wiped us out. But they didn't. They were true gentlemen and they let the score be respectable."

Listening to this story, the more fiery competitor, Jackie, can't help but bring up an example of a defeat that pains her more. "We've had some people run up the score, try to beat us 100 to nothing. That's part of the game for some," she adds. "But it's not the way we play. When you're mismatched, you need to be gracious about it."

*   *   *

Through all sorts of victories and defeats the Murphys say they have learned that the sports they always enjoyed when they were younger have even more value in later years. "A lot of people go down hill once they stop working. It's almost as if they stop living. But I'm going back to the things I enjoyed when I was a kid, and I'm finding that I enjoy them just as much now."

There literally is not enough time in each day for all of the avocations Jackie pursues in her retirement. She delights in quilting, crafts, painting, and cross-stitching. "I don't worry that it has to be something very important, or even something I do very well," she laughs, pointing out a painting that many might consider rudimentary.

"I try to remember that the craft, or the activity I am doing doesn't have to be important," explains Jackie. "That's not the point. The point is that I'm doing something I really enjoy, really love to do. This is why I don't understand people who won't try new things. What's the worst that could happen? It won't turn out to be perfect. So what? Life is precious and it is short enough as it is. Why wait to enjoy things?"

＊　　　＊　　　＊

As Jackie and Arthur describe their experiences in sports and in their hobbies they always seem to return to the happy state of being lost in an activity. They say they feel fully focused, physically attuned, undistracted, and energized.

"You still have all your troubles in the background but for the time being, you are lost to the world," says Jackie.

"We are traveling, meeting new people, and learning new things all the time. On a good day I find myself noticing how late it is and saying to myself, 'Where did the day go?'" says Arthur. "That's when I know I am having a really good time."

In the end the goal, for Arthur and Jackie, is to have fun. "Kids and family have been first in our lives, but now that we have the time to ourselves we are going back to a lot of the things we enjoyed when we were young," says Jackie. "Every day there's a reason to get up and get going." "We're not put on this earth to be miserable," adds Arthur.

*   *   *

Not satisfied to simply enjoy what they have learned about life, the Murphys believe in passing on some of their wisdom about the simple pleasures of life. On a recent visit to a cracked old shuffleboard court at a public park the Murphys were approached by two young teens.

"They came over and asked about the game," recalls Arthur. "They had never seen it before."

"You know what they said?" adds Jackie. "They said, 'How come you old people get all the good games?'"

The Murphys laughed and then made the boys an offer. "Come back tomorrow morning at nine, and we'll teach you how to play," said Arthur.

Jackie and Arthur kept their part of the bargain, rising early and getting to the park a bit before nine o'clock. When the appointed time arrived, the boys came wheeling up on their bikes. An hour later, they were shuffleboard players. "They loved doing it," says Arthur. And so did the Murphys.

AL SIMMONS

Always an Athlete

Life in Harlem was far from easy during the Post-Depression years when Al Simmons was growing up there.

"Money was tight; we had no television. Sports was it, our outlet. Stickball in the street was a big favorite. I first learned to swim in the East River and over on the West Side off 125th Street. The water was dirty, but we didn't pay that any mind," said Simmons.

When he could afford the 11-cent entry fee, Simmons swam at the public pool.

Now, the 65-year-old retiree, of Roosevelt, Long Island, NY man swims three mornings a week in the pristine waters of the Nassau County Aquatic Center, the scene of the regional Senior Olympics swim meets.

*　　　*　　　*

As far back as Simmons can recall, sports have played a pivotal role in his life. He was captain of the DeWitt Clinton High School basketball team, went on to play basketball on a scholarship in college, and later in the U.S Army Special Services while stationed in Greenland during the Korean War. He spent 33 years teaching physical education in the New York City public school system, and all the while coached basketball teams and swim teams.

At 6' and 195 pounds, Simmons appears fit and younger than his years. He is not much heavier than he was in his Army days. Still, he shies away from more than an occasional game of basketball for fear of injury. Swimming and walking afford him the safe exercise he feels he needs.

"Once you're an athlete you're always an athlete, no matter what. Even if you're just sitting down watching a basketball game. It's conversation..., good, healthy conversation."

❉   ❉   ❉

Fellow swimmers that Simmons has met during his early morning swims, form the nucleus of a like-minded group of friends he has made at the pool. They share many a conversation about their common interest in all sorts of sports.

"Sports are fun," he added. They take you away from the everyday stressful routine." Simmons recalls that his father, a teamster and union leader, was an excitable man with a mercurial temperament. The elder Simmons died of a stroke while giving an impassioned speech at a union hall. By contrast, his son has always turned to sports as a way of letting off steam.

And, as an African-American, Simmons is no stranger to the tensions, anger, and frustrations brought about by racial discrimination.

"Yes, it was there," he said of the bias he has been subject to, particularly in college and in his early job-hunting days. "But other ethnic groups have had to deal with it as well. You learn from it and you move on. There are opportunities and you take them. You don't lean on the past."

*   *   *

Both Al and his wife of 40 years, Arneta, taught in the New York City public school system before retiring. That, after Simmons found that racial biases blocked him from pursuing his earlier chosen career of accounting.

The Simmonses have two adult sons, both in the professions and both off on their own. Like their father, they are strong athletes who swim and play basketball.

"Dad's formula seems to be working for them," said their proud father. "I'm still around, and I set the pace. They watch, and they follow, and that's the way it should be."

Neither Al nor Arneta smokes or drinks. Al, in fact, has never smoked because of his commitment to sports. In recent years they have begun to follow a careful but not restricted diet, preferring vegetables, not too much salt, and no fried foods.

Fortunately, both enjoy excellent health, and Simmons credits participation in sports for a good part of that. Arneta took part in sports and was a cheerleader in her school days.

"We've made it," said Simmons. At the senior swim meets he looks to the participants he sees there who are in their eighties and even their nineties as role models. And, while she probably can't swim a stroke, he also admires Lena Horne as a role model who remains attractive and active in the face of advancing years.

Simmons has accumulated a box of first place medals and ribbons for both the 50-yard and 100-yard freestyle and breaststroke events. He recalls taking part in the Senior Olympic Nationals in Florida last year as a high point he wishes all seniors could share.

"There were people in the stadium from various states. It was a moment of joy. We could participate in a big event. It's not over for people our age. It reminded me of the Super Bowl. I can see the Senior Olympics really mushrooming. It's like the real Olympics."

Exercise, particularly in his case, swimming, puts seniors in "a whole new world; it puts you in a different mode. We can't lean on the fact that we're old and we can't do."

"We can't give it up. We can never give it up to the day we die. And we just hope there's some sports activity wherever we go after that...up or down."

LINDA VAN VALKENBURG

Girls Play Sports

When Linda Van Valkenburg was a little girl, her parents refused to buy her sports equipment, because "girls don't play sports."

So Linda borrowed her older brother's bat, ball and glove, saved her pennies to buy her own, and grew up to become a physical education teacher.

A few years back, when a torn Achilles tendon put Van Valkenburg in a large cast and a wheelchair for nearly 7 months, she marked the removal of the cast by driving the wheelchair to the edge of a nearby swimming pool and diving in. That was the beginning of her rehabilitation, which she herself supervised.

When it comes to sports, the woman is determined.

Now, at age 55, Van Valkenburg is a participant in the Senior Olympic Games.

Her sports include softball, for which she has organized and manages her own team, as well as the shot put, discus throw, and table tennis. She intends to add the 100-

meter dash, and perhaps volleyball. Her main problem will be the logistics, fitting in all the events at the competition, because some are scheduled at the same time.

*   *   *

Born in the Bronx, Van Valkenburg still calls that borough home. Divorced and the mother of an adult son, she has taught physical education in the New York City schools for the past 32 years, and more recently has also served as a dean. She plans to retire next year.

"And when I do, I'm ready for the next phase of my life. The Senior Games will be a big part of it because I enjoy it," says Van Valkenburg.

"Recently a former neighbor of mine passed away just shy of his 102nd birthday. I would go to visit him in the nursing home. I'd see these people sitting in the hallways, many just bobbing their heads, no interest in anything, just waiting to die. Then I'd go to the Senior Games and I'd see people the same age keeping active, running around, having a ball, strong, enjoying life. That's the way I want to go," she adds.

Three years ago, Van Valkenburg attended a reunion at her alma mater, Hunter College. A chance meeting there led her to the Games.

"A former teacher said, 'You must be 50 by now, why don't you join the Senior Games, they have all sorts of sports.'"

Today that former teacher, who is 68, along with yet another former Hunter College teacher and coach, age 79, both play on the softball team Van Valkenburg has organized.

"They're my role models. They're still doing it. It's the ones who keep doing it who stay healthy. They won't end up in a nursing home," she explains.

Prior to organizing her own softball team, Van Valkenburg was part of a Senior Games softball team based in Schenectady. The distance made it impossible for her to attend practices; so she arranged to practice locally and joined up with her team when they competed at the NYS Olympics.

Meanwhile the group she played with locally included women in their twenties, thirties, and forties. Age, however, was no problem.

"There's a certain amount of respect you get when you

hit the ball over the fence, no matter what your age," she says. Actually, Van Valkenburg had never hit the ball out of the park until she reached the age of 50.

She enjoys the camaraderie of the Senior Games almost as much as the sport itself.

"It's great. At the national competition you meet people from all over the country. You have a sport in common with them, and they're like old friends. You network with people from all over."

*　　　*　　　*

Like many Senior Olympians, Van Valkenburg prizes a cap, which she has decorated with pins from other states. She carries a bag of New York State pins to trade as she goes. Each pin she trades for seems to have a story behind it. Of particular interest is the pin from New Mexico, which she picked up at the National Games in Orlando.

"I got it from a 99-year-old Navajo Indian who was in the archery competition. He scored a Gold despite being confined to a wheelchair. We traded state pins and I took a picture with him."

The pins provide a talking point for her students back home.

"I show them my cap and my medals and ribbons. I tell them they can do this throughout their whole lives. It's motivating for them. On open-school night one girl asked me to show my medals to her dad," says Van Valkenburg.

*   *   *

While it hardly seems necessary for her to get any more physical exercise than she's already getting, Van Valkenburg does her own stretching routine each morning to "maintain flexibility, range of motion, and just get me ready for the day." She also uses hand weights and feels if she were to let her routine lapse for more than three days, her muscles would start to atrophy.

"I belong to a gym and try to get my friends to come there with me, but I have to drag them along," she said. She finds that going to the gym energizes her even when she feels tired. She has been using the padded gym at the high school where she teaches to practice the shot put and the discus. But she's improved to the point that she's been hitting the walls, so she's moving outside to the field at Lehman College.

*   *   *

Van Valkenburg is tall and of average build. She maintains her weight, despite being on what she calls the "see food diet... I see food and I eat it." Most of her friends, by comparison, are on perpetual diets, and continue to gain weight.

Along with the competition and excitement of the Senior Olympic Games, there are the social events.

"When we were in Syracuse for the State Games they held a big dance. It was fun. I remember an 89-year-old cyclist there; he danced every dance. There are a number of social activities. The people are excited about it and it's really nice."

Back in the Bronx, Van Valkenburg keeps contact with some of the people she's met through the games by phone and via e-mail. She was delighted one day to receive some photographs of herself receiving a medal that were taken by another participant from Chicago. The photos are right there with her fast-growing collection of pins, medals and ribbons.

JIMMIE HARGROVE

Faith, Love, and Bowling

Jimmie Hargrove may be the only lady named Jimmie for a hundred miles around, but she's proud of her name. It came directly from her father, who took care of a family of four by working more than forty hard years as a track laborer for the Illinois Central Railroad.

Born in 1931 in Greenwood, Mississippi, Jimmie attended a tiny elementary school — a segregated school for blacks only — where each room held more than one grade. At the start of each year she and her brother were almost alone because most of the other children lived on farms and were needed for the harvest.

"My dad didn't want to work in the fields and he didn't want us to, either. That's why he joined the railroad and stayed with it no matter how hard it was," she recalls with pride. "But he wasn't all serious. He had a lot of fun, and he taught us to work hard but also enjoy everything that life had to offer."

Jimmie Hargrove's father was the main influence in her life, she says. "He was very relaxed about things. He said you should let go of all the small things that bother you, and then, when you decide to do something that's important to you, give it your all." By his example, Jimmie Hargrove's father taught her about the power of love. She adds, "You have to love people. Some of them may make themselves awfully difficult to love," she jokes. "But you got to love them anyway."

*   *   *

Sports and outdoor activities were always part of Jimmie Hargrove's life. Still 5'9" at age 67, she is trim and very strong, just as she was as a girl. "I was always with my brother and his friends," she says. "I climbed trees, hopped fences, played ball, and went fishing in the Mississippi River. We caught some big catfish back then."

Today Jimmie Hargrove still loves to fish, and she remains passionate about sport. She attends professional baseball, football, and basketball games. Every year she goes to the Superbowl with a huge group of people from her tiny hometown. She walks a mile-and-a-half every day. And she competes regularly in both miniature golf and her main game, bowling.

"I really started bowling when I moved North, in 1949," says Hargrove. Like millions of African Americans at the time, she left the rural South to find a better paying job and a more exciting life. She found both.

"I worked for a lot of manufacturing companies — making electric motors, hearing aids, communications equipment — and they all had bowling leagues and teams. We played softball too, but I loved bowling."

*　　　*　　　*

Some of the friends that Jimmie Hargrove made while a member of various bowling teams remained friends for life. Along with the members of her church, they became her most stalwart supports during some very trying times. They were there when two of her four children died — one in an auto accident and one from cancer.

"Those kinds of things aren't supposed to happen all to one person," she says. "You aren't supposed to outlive your children. But I have managed to get through with my friends and my faith."

"I believe you have to have a very strong faith in God to endure. I do believe that He has a plan for me. I believe that He will give me all the strength I need. When people say that's not true, or that life really doesn't have meaning, I can't accept that. I think that God puts us here to love each other and to love him. That's something I can do, no matter what is happening."

*   *   *

Jimmie Hargrove's love is expressed in the company of her bowling group and when she competes each year in the Senior Games. "Now those women at the games, they can bowl," she says with genuine admiration. "They have averages in the 170s and 180s. I'm only about 140. But I have a very good doubles partner and when we're together, we do very well. We've gotten medals three out of five times."

Though she is generous in her praise for her opponents and partner, Jimmie is also eager to improve and win gold medals as an individual. "If you let yourself get involved, give in to it, then you start to desire to get better and better. One day I want to be able to say that I am the best at this and get the Gold. I've always felt that way when playing sports. I am a competitive person and I have that urge to win."

Like many fit seniors, Jimmie Hargrove eats a well-balanced diet. She doesn't drink "because I saw how goofy it makes people." And she doesn't smoke. But she doesn't mention any of these elements of her lifestyle when she reflects on the qualities that have made her a happy, active senior athlete. Instead, Jimmie focuses on the role played by courage. "The Bible says that as soon as you are born, you are on your way to dying, but there's nothing to fear in that. Well, if death's not something to fear, then why should I be afraid of anything?"

"I think a lot of people are so afraid to fail that they cannot work up the courage to try. If you don't try, you haven't given yourself the chance to succeed. No one succeeds at anything without first experiencing failure, but it's worth it."

Sport, and the courage that lies behind it, have given Hargrove a vibrant life despite her many losses. She sees a relationship between her bowling and the social contacts it brings, and her continued vitality. And she guards the time she devotes to them fiercely.

"I have fifteen grandchildren and there's a tradition in African- American families of the grandmother always taking care of the grandchildren. Well, I'll help out if I'm really needed, but I'm not one of those handing over my life to that. Too many grandparents do that. My children need to take care of their own responsibilities as parents and I have my own life to live. I'm always going to be going out and doing something. You're never too old for that."

II

Wavemakers

All competitive athletes, whether they face off against an opponent or just try to achieve a new personal best, eventually express a certain fearlessness. They are determined to assert their minds, bodies, and spirits. If this means making a few waves, they are not afraid to do it. Some athletes, like Herm Arrow, have always been wavemakers. Others, like Lillian Creno, actually acquire a sense of fearlessness through their sport. All of them are comfortable with expressing who they are in any arena.

LILLIAN CRENO

Strong as a Horse

Lillian Creno vividly recalls the way her father woke her up during the vacation she spent at Flint Lake in Indiana when she was eight-years old. He would toss her bathing suit — still wet — onto her face. She would roll over and complain, and then smile. In a matter of minutes she and her sister Jeanne would be in the lake.

Sixty-eight years later, Lillian Creno can still cut through the water with both grace and speed. She is still thrilled by the competition of racing, and she revels in the way her body feels in the water.

"I feel strong, and I feel connected to the person I've always been," explains Lillian. "I am pretty confident in the water, and that's a very nice feeling."

*   *   *

Unlike senior athletes who come to sports later in life, Lillian Creno can claim a connection to training and competition that goes back as far as she can remember. Her father, an accomplished swimmer and semi-pro football player, taught his daughters to love water during their first vacation at Flint Lake. Lillian and Jeanne loved the attention he lavished on them, and swam hard.

"We didn't swim across the lake," recalls Lillian. "We swam all the way around the lake. My dad would row a boat around following us."

A natural athlete, Lillian played soccer and baseball in school, but swimming was her passion. She and her sister shined in competitions at small clubs around Chicago and were soon recruited by the prestigious Lake Shore Club. They were given free memberships and became key members of teams that won several national amateur championships.

"Winning was in our blood from the very beginning," explains Lillian. "The first time I lost was when I was twelve, and I entered a really big meet sponsored by the Chicago Tribune. I got second place, and I cried and cried. My father scolded me, and he was right. I learned that losing is part of it and that I had to be a good sport."

Lillian devoted herself to swimming all through her school years. After graduating high school she went to work for the Illinois Central Railroad, where wartime manpower shortages meant that she rose quickly within the company. Though she couldn't train as much, she swam every night and continued to participate with the Lake Shore team, swimming backstroke, freestyle, and relays.

The Creno sisters raced, but were better known as teammates in synchronized swimming events. In 1944 they appeared in Life magazine. In 1948, while Lillian had dropped out of competition after getting married, Jeanne went to the Olympics.

"We both benefited so much from athletics," explains Lillian. "I mean, I think our parents thought that it was a good way to keep us occupied with something positive during those years when kids get in a lot of trouble. But it also taught me a lot about life. You learn the principle of fair play. You get a very good idea of how you respond to a challenge. And you find out that hard work pays off."

*   *   *

Lillian dropped out of competitive swimming when the young man she loved — he had been a lifeguard at Lake Flint — came home from World War II, and they were married. Ernest and Lillian Creno had two sons who became athletes themselves; and though she took breaks to raise them, Lillian was never long out of the workforce. In those jobs she applied the values she had learned in the pool: hard work, fair play.

"I worked for 48 years," she says proudly. "I worked for three different law firms and two universities. It was sometimes very hard to get along with the people in those places. They had very strong personalities. But I had been on teams, and knew how to work with anyone."

Long after dropping out of competition, Lillian continued to swim for pleasure and to keep physically fit. She credits this habit with the remarkably good health she has enjoyed her entire life. She believes that she also benefited from not smoking and from a moderate diet that excludes both alcohol and excessive amounts of sugar. "I've never had a bottle of pop in my life," she says. Genetics are probably on her side too. Her mother lived to age 90 and was quite active to the end.

Though she had never imagined returning to the pool in pursuit of medals, when Lillian Creno first heard about the Arizona Senior Games (she had by then moved there from the Midwest), she immediately felt the desire to sign up. "I was working at Arizona State University, and the Games were being held there. Deciding to participate was one of the best things I ever did."

In the years that followed, Lillian Creno participated in every single one of the State Games and qualified to represent Arizona in the Nationals as well. "It is wonderful for many reasons. The first is you get to meet so many nice people. We have the same interests, wanting to do something good for ourselves, to keep active and busy."

As she talks about the Arizona teams that have gone to national meets, Lillian begins to sound a little like the girl who swam in Chicago so long ago. "The Nationals are a higher level of competition, which is wonderful," she says. "But you have just as much fun going around watching the other people compete in their sports. We all know all the kids, and we get a kick out of supporting each other. There's one 90-year-old runner who can really move. We love watching him."

*   *   *

Though the Senior Games sometimes makes Lillian Creno feel like a kid again, she can become quite serious when she describes a benefit that others haven't mentioned. "The fact is, when you are in your seventies, you have to know that health problems might be right around the corner."

In Lillian's case, a health crisis struck her husband, Ernest, first. He recently suffered a stroke; and though he's substantially recovered, she has had to care for him in ways she never anticipated.

"He once fell down in the front yard, and a jogger came by and saw him lying there," recalls Lillian. "He told him, 'Ring the bell. Get my wife. She's strong as a horse.'"

Lillian was able to come out, help her husband up, and take care of him. Most other women of 76 years would have been hard-pressed to do it.

"The point is, being in sports has been good for me, and it also makes me strong to help others. I guess I am as strong as a horse, and that's a good thing for a lot of reasons."

HERM ARROW

A Side Order of Humor

Herm Arrow came of age in perilous times. When the stock market crashed in 1929, he was nine—old enough to understand what it meant, especially to his mother and father who owned a small grocery store. His adolescence was scarred by The Great Depression. But as a student at Lincoln High School in Brooklyn, he was most affected by the rise in fascism around the world. After 60 years, the feelings he experienced then are still strong.

"During the '30s we lived through what was happening in Germany, Spain, and Italy, and it made a real impression on me," recalls Herm. "I became very aware of other people's struggles, and of how all our lives were connected. It also made me realize that life is precious, and you should never just stand on the sidelines. I have felt ever since that every day is valuable."

Driven by his conviction that every moment of life has real value, Herm found outlets in both his work and his avocations. He fell in love with photography, studied it in school, and worked for several years as a professional. Later when he went into the wine business in California, he held on to his art as well as his love for classical music, continuing to make pictures as an expression of what was in his heart.

But as so many men of his generation did, Arrow poured most of his energy into his work. Through the 1960s and 1970s he was right in the center of the boom in the California wine business. "The stress was high and constant," he explains. "I worked for Gallo as a sales manager, and the saying then was, 'If you can work for Gallo, you can handle working for anyone.'"

The hard-driving life that Herm Arrow experienced was, no doubt, a factor in the heart disease that literally laid him out in 1986. He underwent a quadruple by-pass operation that changed his heart in more ways than one. "If I wanted to live, I was going to have to adopt a much different lifestyle," says Herm. "And I definitely wanted to live."

Arrow retired from the wine business. He and his wife Lois became vegetarians and began to exercise regularly. In his search for an aerobic activity that was good for his heart and easy on his joints and muscles, Herm settled on race walking. It would be a fateful choice.

"For several years I did it on my own, developing my own technique from looking at pictures, reading, and watching race walkers. Then eight years ago I joined the Marin Race Walkers, a club for people who do it all the time. My primary interest was staying healthy, but we have a coach, Jack Bray, who was a national champion, and he was able to teach me a great deal."

With Bray's coaching, Herm Arrow gained the speed, endurance, and confidence to enter Senior Games competitions. Soon he was winning races and medals, including 2 bronze and 1 silver medal (1996-1997-1998) at the U.S.A. Track & Field National Masters Championships and gold and silver medals in the 1998 California State Senior Olympics Games.

For some, becoming a senior athlete means re-discovering a love for sport they enjoyed long ago. For Herm Arrow, it was an introduction to an aspect of life he had never known. Except for playing a little handball in his teenage years, he had not been an athletic kid. Indeed, his interests had always been primarily intellectual: photography, music, politics. Suddenly, in his seventh decade of life, he was a fiercely competitive athlete.

"The competition is very exciting, and I love to win medals," says Arrow. Each year's schedule of races gives Herm a series of goals to look forward to and they add purpose to his daily training. "Age does slow a racer down," says Arrow. So the younger men in each age category — his is now the 80 to 85 group — do have an advantage. "I just turned 80, so I'm the kid again in my group," he laughs.

Racing in national meets has also brought Herm Arrow friendships that span the country. "There may be only ten of us nationally who are really competitive in this age group," he explains. "I know all of the others, and we all want to win. I know I want to compete and succeed more and more as I realize that I have less time on this earth to enjoy."

This ever-growing appreciation for life's value is also one of the motivations for his volunteer work with an organization called Mended Hearts. Affiliated with the American Heart Association, Mended Hearts brings survivors of heart disease together with people who have been diagnosed with similar problems. The members of the group visit patients who have had heart attacks or heart surgery.

"A lot of the patients can relate better to us than to a nurse or doctor who has never been lying in that bed," says Arrow. "We are given training in how to say the right thing. But it makes a big impression when they see us bouncing in and showing that you can have a very full, active life after heart disease." He strongly recommends getting involved in a sport or a creative activity, "anything that gives you feedback for your efforts."

In the 15 years since his heart surgery, Arrow has reached several conclusions about his own illness and recovery. He believes that two major factors — a genetic predisposition and diet — contributed to the development of his heart disease. "Just about everyone in my family died of heart disease, and what we ate was heavy foods loaded with fat," he explains.

On the recovery side of the ledger, Arrow lists: improved diet, vigorous exercise, stress reduction, loving relationships, and a sense of humor. The last two may be the most important.

"My wife and I are very close, very supportive of each other," he reports. "And I can also tell you that aging doesn't mean giving up on making love. That's still there."

"In the banquet of life, perhaps the most important side order is humor," adds Arrow. He advises that a whimsical attitude can make even the most frightening moments in life bearable. As an example, he offers an incident that he recently survived.

"I take a lot of vitamins and herbs, maybe six or seven capsule or tablets with each meal," he explains. "I was at a restaurant, and I took my vitamins with a sip of water from a straw. One of the vitamins got stuck pretty good. I ate a little bread to try to push it down, but that only made it worse."

Arrow signaled his distress to his wife, and soon a large man from a nearby table was hugging him from behind and using the Heimlich maneuver to dislodge the bread and vitamin. "I was really frightened and very relieved," recalls Arrow. "I'm sure I looked pale and shaky, but as I sat down, a funny thing ran through my head. It was a newspaper headline that said, 'World-Class Athlete Chokes to Death on Vitamin.' Now that would be a funny headline."

Funny as it may be, Arrow is in no hurry for any kind of headline announcing his departure from this Earth. "I have too much to enjoy in life. My relationships, helping others through Mended Hearts, competing, training. All of it feels good. Every morning I go to train at a track where there is a wonderful view of a mountain, Mt. Tam. And every morning I say, 'Good morning Mt. Tam, I'm here again today.' I hope to say that many, many more times."

JANE SMITH

Un-plain Jane

Perhaps the only thing commonplace about Jane Smith is her name. Other than that, the 65 year old Long Island woman is the mother of 10, the grandmother of 19, a nurse volunteer, a medallist in swimming, and a woman who keeps a wet suit in the closet for those times when she goes windsurfing in the Great South Bay.

Jane Smith is not anyone's typical grandmother.

She first became seriously interested in swimming while in her fifties and working as a nurse in a prison in North Carolina, where the family lived at the time.

"Every day I passed a "Y" on my way home. I would stop to take a swim just to keep my body from falling apart," says Smith.

While still in North Carolina, she learned about the local Senior Games.

"At that point I was old enough,' you had to be 55. I signed up thinking it would be enjoyable to try. They told me I had qualified for the state games. But I was afraid to go. I felt I wasn't a good enough swimmer. So I just did the local games for a couple of years. Then, one of my daughters said she would go with me to the State Games in Raleigh. She was my cheerleader. And then I was eligible for the National Games."

After some cajoling, Jane's husband Gerry accompanied his wife to the 1997 National Senior Games in Arizona (Eventually he would join in the play, too, winning a bronze medal in basketball in the year 2000.)

"We did go and we had a wonderful time. It's just a spirit that you can't describe to people. It's exciting. We wore tags that didn't say 'Senior Citizen' or anything; they said 'Athlete', and I was so impressed with that. And you met so many people who were just good sports and so full of life. And whether they won or lost they just gave off a positive spirit. We had such a good time and we've continued with it."

Now Jane also swims in other meets. She competes primarily in the breaststroke and some freestyle, and has the medals to show for it.

"At a recent meet, we had a man 90 years old, who broke two world records while he was there. It was so embarrassing. I swam in the same heat he did in one of the races, and this little old man, who had recently fractured his hip and had six pins in it, beat me!"

*   *   *

At home Jane swims with a group of women 65 to 69 years of age. But she marvels at another group of women swimmers who are older.

"The next block of swimmers has some super women. A lot of these people swam in college and they have continued. They're a good example for the rest of us, who are just plodding," she says. She considers the swimmers who are 75, 80, even 90 years of age as role models. "I look at these people who are getting out and doing things. They're marvelous," she says.

Not everyone understands. Jane says some of her friends have difficulty understanding her commitment. "They ask me why I would do that. For instance, I get up at 5:30 AM to swim over at the school. You have to go when the kids aren't there and the pools are available."

Smith has been trying to convince a group of women friends to join her, but they are turned off when they hear about the early hour at which the pools are open.

She, however, goes at least three times a week.

"It makes me feel good. Very good. It's a time when you're all by yourself. There's no telephones ringing. Nobody can bother you. You can just let your mind wander. I find it almost a healing thing. It's no strain on your body; it's just very pleasant. You're not jarring your hips or ankles or your knees."

Smith is 5'9," lean, long, and attractive. She wears no make-up, but her skin exudes a healthy glow. Aside from swimming, she works out with weights to keep her muscles strong. She'll tell you that a soccer accident when she was in her forties damaged her knee and keeps her from pursuing what she considers other strenuous sports.

But then you notice the sports equipment catalogue on the table and it's open to the windsurfing equipment. So who goes windsurfing?

"Well, I do that occasionally," she says. "Of course, I can't fly over the waves like some of the younger people do." Still, she is serious enough about the sport to have a carrier atop her car and a wet suit handy in the closet.

*   *   *

Smith's immediate family members...all 30 of them ...are extremely supportive of her efforts. Her four daughters and six sons have a keen interest in sports. One daughter is a nationally ranked tri-athlete. Husband Gerry is a retired teacher and athletic coach.

"They're very proud that their old mother does this," says Smith.

At home Jane and Gerry follow a sensible diet without concentrating much on it. Both enjoy good health. Together they do a lot of walking. She often takes a nap in the afternoon to assure she's able to wake before sunrise for her workout at the pool.

While Smith is retired from her profession of nursing, she continues to use her knowledge and experience by working as a volunteer at a hospice for people in the terminal stages of AIDS. Despite her success in the water, she still gets butterflies before a meet.

"I dread getting up on the starting block. I'll get nauseated and dizzy. I worry about my goggles falling off. But then I tell myself, nobody's going to know I'm there, and I just try to finish the race. But every time there's a meet I worry about silly things like the goggles or making a false start."

And it's worth it?

"Oh, yes, when it's all over, it's so good. You did it," she says.

Recently, an old friend phoned Smith to say that she is training to get back into running, which she used to do competitively.

"Here we are, both 65 and we're planning on our future. It's a very positive thing. We're lucky and we should make the best of what we've got. You've got to leave this world a little bit better place," says Smith.

ARTHUR COSTELLO

The Shy Medallist

"When he grows up, he aspires to be like those guys who are 80 and 85 years old who still participate in sports," says Beverly Costello.

She is referring to her husband Arthur and his participation in the swimming events in the Senior Olympics. Costello is 71, but anyone would be hard pressed to believe he's a day over 60.

While Costello says he is not a dedicated swimmer, he underestimates himself. This is a man who learned to swim as a kid at The Bathhouse in Harlem, a NYC Parks Department indoor pool at 134th Street. He later worked as a lifeguard for the New York Parks Department and played water polo in college.

Over the years Costello has continued to swim with The Dolphin Senior Group, at the Roy Wilkins Family Center in Jamaica, Queens. It was there that Costello first heard about the Senior Games; at the time he was 65.

Nowadays, Costello continues to swim at the Wilkins Center and tries to put in three mornings a week in the pool at Echo Park near his West Hempstead, Long Island home. He plans to be at the Nassau County Games as well as the State Games in Syracuse. His events are the 50 and 100-yard freestyle, and he's got a sizable collection of medals and ribbons that prove his dedication, despite his claim to the contrary.

Costello is a survivor. But, it's only with the advancing years that he's begun to think of himself as such. Just recently he has begun to fully realize the benefits he's gained from his lifelong participation in swimming, as well as skiing, roller skating, ice skating, tennis, and bowling.

*   *   *

"When I was younger, I wasn't worried about health. It's just since I retired that I reflect back and realize that the longevity in my family has been short. I'm surprised I'm still here," said Costello.

Costello's father succumbed to cancer at the age of 45. His mother died at 56 with high blood pressure; and his two siblings, a brother and a sister, have also passed away. None of them was sports-minded.

Beverly Costello accompanies her husband when he

goes out of town to participate in the Games. This is a second marriage for both, and they glow in each other's company. Between them they now share five children, eight grandchildren, and a youthful zest for living rarely seen in a couple who are 71 and 69 respectively. Both are retired; he is a former New York City fireman, she is a former music teacher in the New York City school system.

When Arthur last participated in the State Games, Beverly traveled Upstate with a troupe that entertained the participants with a line dancing routine. Line dancing is something Beverly does regularly for fundraisers and parties.

Ever shy about his accomplishments, Arthur refrains from mentioning that he and Beverly, together, have won a number of ballroom dance competitions. Dance trophies are scattered throughout the living room of the Costello home.

The couple recommends the Senior Games as a means of socializing. While they attend the state competitions with a large local contingent, they also meet people from other areas.

"There are barbecues, jazz singers, a major banquet. It's

so alive some people go for the socialization even if they're not involved in the games," said Beverly. "They are spectators, friends, family. There are plenty of things to do for which there are no medals; and things that have nothing to do with sports, such as a Scrabble competition." She herself may join in the 5-kilometer speed-walk or perhaps the "prediction walk," in which participants predict how far they will walk.

As far as the competitive events go, Costello said people get "pumped up."

"It's exciting. The medals are not important. Just being there is important. Some people come in last, but everybody is hollering for them just to finish. It's not to win so much as it's to be in it."

Costello is considering expanding his participation. He may add the long jump and the high jump to the events in which he already competes.

*   *   *

From day to day the Costellos follow a fairly active exercise routine. Beverly does aerobic exercises and a great deal of walking in addition to all the line dancing. Arthur exercises each morning.

He does the cooking and the couple tends to eat lean foods. They keep a "weight book" and have an official weighing in, which is recorded in the book on the first Tuesday of every month. The routine began when Arthur had put on a few extra pounds, which he has now removed. (Arthur is 6' and weighs 195. Beverly is small and slender and her weight hardly fluctuates at all.)

Costello said he tries to encourage friends in his age group to get involved in physical activity. But at the same time warns them that being "too active" could lead to trouble. As for himself, he said, "As long as I can be involved with swimming, I'll always do it. Even if I can only walk in the water."

III

Iron Men

The Gulf Coast of Florida is the home of what may be the best-known tri-atholon club in the world, the St. Pete Mad Dogs. The Mad Dogs support and sponsor hundreds of athletes who participate worldwide in races that require a long distance swim, a longer run, and an even longer bicycle ride.

Remarkably, well over a dozen of the Mad Dogs are over age 65. They train and compete with club members of all ages. Many enter Iron Man competitions, in which they must cover more than 100 miles on the water, by bike, and on foot. They also serve as examples and inspiration for anyone who wonders just how much a senior athlete can do.

JIM WARD

Iron Man

Jim Ward tries to disarm you, to make you believe that he was once a perfectly ordinary young man. "The only team I ever made was the debate team," he says with a laugh. "I liked sports, but I also liked girls and going out with my friends. But I did notice one thing. I had a lot of energy and endurance."

Energy and endurance would prove to be the foundation of Jim Ward's life. In fact, one day they would probably mean the difference between life and death. But there's one other quality that Ward fails to mention in his rambling effort to explain why, at age 83, he can run, bike, and swim with people half his age: Strength of character.

It was evident, back at Malden (Massachusetts) High School when Ward joined the debate team that he now mentions in jest. It wasn't just any debate team. It was the oldest high school debate team in the nation. And at the time, the early 1930s, it operated by rules that excluded blacks and Jews. Ward made it his business to challenge, and then overturn those rules.

"Intolerance is, to me, a terrible thing," explains Ward. "In fact, I have always believed that tolerance and integrity are the keys to character."

Jim Ward was not simply tolerant of human differences, he was absolutely fascinated by all the colors and flavors of human experience, and by the ways people manage to live together amid these differences. "In Boston, you inhale the air and you are infected by politics," he recalls. "And for two years there I lectured on sight-seeing busses." That experience fed his interest in the drama of life.

The eldest of seven children, Ward was a paratrooper in World War II. Dropped behind enemy lines in Burma, he helped lead a contingent of Kachin tribesmen fighting the Japanese. Though he contracted both malaria and dysentery, he survived both, thanks to his body's remarkable durability. Indeed, he covered more than 2,000 miles on foot in Burma without much trouble. By war's end, he was enthralled with the adventure of travel and foreign cultures. He joined the Foreign Service and, in a decision that would prove vital to his long-term health, remained in the Army as a reserve officer.

"I actually think that's where my running took hold," he explains. "I wanted to be in the 82nd Airborne and the Special Forces. In order to do that you had to be able to run five miles. I began training for that reason."

*   *   *

The only marathons in Jim Ward's life in the 1940s, '50s, and '60s, were social marathons. "I was posted in a great many places: Rangoon, Japan, Austria, and Czechoslovakia. But one thing was always the same. On a great many evenings the embassy staff would be invited to two different cocktail parties and then a dinner party. You would stay out very late and then get up early to start working. I always noticed that I could do this without much problem while everyone else was exhausted. I began to think that while I never had much speed or coordination, I really did have endurance."

Ward's endurance was tested when he was posted in South Vietnam at the height of America's war against the North Vietnamese. Even as the war effort was grinding on, Ward could see the flaws in the strategy. "It was never primarily a military conflict," he explains. "It was a political conflict, and if we had gone in with massive economic aid to help the local people we might have done much better."

As tragic as the Vietnam conflict was for all of America,

it was even more tragic for Ward. All of his professional effort was for naught, and his only son, paratrooper James Patrick Ward, was killed in action. "I tried to tell him to go to college, but he wouldn't have it," recalls Ward. "He had grown up in countries with communism and he thought it was a terrible thing. He believed in what he was doing."

   *   *   *

Having survived two wars and the loss of his son, Jim Ward entered retirement wondering if he would spend much of his time in a rocking chair with a good book. He expected a long life. After all, his mother lived to age 93 in good health. But he had no idea that it would be as physically vital as it turned out to be.

"At age 65, I read a book by a Dr. Kenneth Cooper on the benefits of aerobic exercise," he recalls. Ward began running with a more serious purpose: extending and energizing his life. Soon he discovered that he could enter races for seniors where he would be matched against men his own age. "I ran in the Boston Marathon, the Marine Corps Marathon, and the Las Vegas Marathon." With each of these experiences he acquired new friends. Eventually he found himself part of a large community of senior runners. He also became a sort of evangelist for the benefits of aerobic exercise, which rushes oxygen through the body.

"The human body needs air, food, and water," adds Ward. "We can go five days without water, and five weeks without food. But we can't go five minutes without air. That's how important it is."

After studying both health and longevity, Ward identified a few keys to both. A balanced diet that is low on sugar and fat is important, he says. (Ward does not frequent McDonald's and he eats plenty of vegetables.) But diet is not nearly as important to him as vigorous aerobic exercise. "The minimum for any benefit is twenty minutes, five times per week," he says. Of course, he far exceeds the minimum.

*   *   *

"I started triathlons when some of my friends got into it," says Ward. He was 68 years old at the time. "The combination of running, swimming and bicycling appealed to me. You never get bored."

The triathlon is the perfect challenge for an athlete whose main asset is stamina. The races can last eighteen hours, and call for swims as long as 2.4 miles, bike rides that can cover 112 miles, and runs that will take competitors over a course of 26 miles. These were the distances that Ward covered in Hawaii at one of the first extreme triathlons — called the Iron Man — which he has completed.

Two years ago, at age 80, Jim Ward encountered his first serious health crisis after he returned home from winning the world championship in his age group in Perth, Australia. "A tiny blood clot that probably came from a bike accident caused a stroke," he recalls. "For 18 hours the left side of my body was paralyzed. Normally they don't give someone my age the advanced drugs they use to treat strokes, but a doctor at the hospital was also a tri-athlete and he knew me. He said I wasn't too old, and they gave it to me."

With the help of this early treatment, Ward's paralysis was short-lived. Within a couple of weeks he was able to run and swim. He followed a rigorous rehabilitation plan, with special attention paid to his left eye, which suffered from some nerve damage. Two years later, he is fully recovered and back in training with a group of elder tri-athletes, both male and female.

"On a typical morning a group of us will get out there at 7 AM and ride twenty miles. We might then go out to breakfast together. The group is important. It's important to have friends and family, people you love, who support you and who you care about too." When he's not biking, Ward can often be found running near his home on the Florida Gulf Coast, or swimming in the Gulf of Mexico.

To remain mentally sharp, he recently joined the local chapter of Toastmasters, an organization that helps members develop public speaking skills. "They'll give you a topic to prepare something on, or you'll participate in a table topic, where they go around the table and ask each person to offer something for a few minutes."

In joining Toastmasters Jim Ward intentionally sought to challenge himself and open himself to new experiences. This open attitude is, he suspects, one of the secrets to a long, vigorous life. "We're living thirty years longer than our great grandparents did," says Ward. "I once asked a doctor what would contribute more to being healthy through that life, genetics or how you live. He said that when you are young, things like power and speed and size are determined by genetics. Maybe 70 percent of your physical ability is genetic at that time."

"But he also said that when you get old, the thing reverses. When you are older, 70 percent is how you live, not what you were born with. That's probably the key. With your diet, exercise, and attitude you have to maximize what you've been born with. I think we can all do that."

ROGER J. BURKE

Finding the Passion

About a quarter mile off shore, Roger J. Burke leads a dozen swimmers, aged 55 to 80, as they stroke from one buoy to another in the warm water of the Gulf of Mexico. A hundred yards away, a pair of dolphins break the surface. They seem to be playing tag. As the humans reach another buoy they stop and gaze at their graceful companions. Roger hollers to the last swimmer to reach the goal.

"Do we go on?" he asks.

This is a group swim. There is nothing competitive about it. The swimmer who is last always decides how far the group will go. But there is enough social pressure here to encourage anyone to swim as far and as hard as he or she can. "Usually they push on," says Burke. This time the older woman who must make the choice does exactly as he predicts. One more buoy. Then another.

"It's how they become stronger. Eventually, that person is no longer the last one. Someone new will come along and it's their turn to get in shape. We take someone who can't swim 25 yards in a backyard pool and get them swimming a whole mile in the Gulf."

Roger Burke's firm, easy-going way of motivating the newcomers in this swim group works miracles with beginners. But it has also propelled him into the top ranks in an athletic event that is one of the most grueling no matter your age: the triathlon. A medal winner at local, regional, and national senior meets, 64-year-old Burke is truly "An Iron Man" among senior athletes. But unlike many others in his sport, he is driven not by the urge to win, but rather, the desire to live life to the fullest.

"I spent a long time focused on making a living," he explains, recalling thirty-three years as a telephone company employee. "Then I retired and focused on making a life. Working out is a big part of that, and I think I'm getting good at it."

*   *   *

Now happily settled on the Gulf Coast of Florida, Roger Burke was born and raised in the New York suburbs. Though he says he barely recalls it, he received a profound and tragic lesson on the value of human life when his mother died of cancer. He was just 8 years old at the time. Then, much later, he watched his father die of heart disease at age 65. His father had only retired a year before.

"My wife and I made a pact," explains Burke. "I was going to take care of myself and retire as soon as possible so we could really enjoy ourselves. I wasn't going to have what happened to my father happen to me." He was already quite healthy and ate a moderate diet. And he stepped up his exercise regimen.

Though he had a demanding job, Burke always found a way to make exercise an important part of his daily routine. He was both determined and ingenious. Consider, for example, the work-out idea that occurred to him as he was stalled in the same traffic jam he sat in every day on his way home from work.

"I pulled off into a residential neighborhood and asked this lady if she would mind if I parked my car in front of her house for a while. It was okay with her. So the next day I brought running clothes to work and changed into them before I got in the car. When I got to that part of the highway I pulled off, parked, and ran the rest of the way home."

Burke covered roughly seven miles on foot, passing thousands of cars that crawled along the road. When he got home, he hopped on a bicycle and took a circuitous route back to fetch his car. All-in-all, he managed to turn the time that everyone else wasted fuming in backed-up traffic to get in a 25-mile workout.

"This is why I don't believe it when people say they don't have time to exercise," he says. "I think you can always make the time. You just have to be creative. You also have to be willing to try something. You can't let that fear of failure prevent you from trying something new."

          *   *   *

The triathlon was completely new to Burke when he took it up in 1985. Until that point he had been an all-around athlete, but he had never thought about participating in a race that involved running, bicycling, and swimming. (Each activity is done over distances ranging from a quarter mile for the swim to more than 100 miles on a bike.) "It was an opportunity to spend time with my son, and try something exciting and challenging," says Burke. "It didn't even occur to me to say no."

The only event that troubled Burke at all was swimming. "That requires real technique, to get the breathing right and the kicking," he explains. "So I had to learn that; but otherwise, it was mostly a matter of training."

Fortunately, Burke loved to train. Indeed, his dozens of medals mean little to him when compared with the benefits of training. "For my health's sake, training is better than anything, and I enjoy it more than racing. I'm just not that competitive that I need to beat other people or win something. To me, it's more about being able to do what I want to do, feeling really good, and having a long, active life. Like I said, I didn't want to make a living, I wanted to make a good life."

*　　　*　　　*

The opportunity to escape "making a living" and find the life he always wanted came as a bit of a surprise. It was 1989 and the news was filled with stories about corporate executives getting "golden parachutes" from companies that were willing to pay them handsomely if they would only retire. In an effort to reduce wages, Burke's employer began making similar deals with lower-level workers who had been on the job long enough to reach fairly high salary levels.

"They came to me with a buy-out offer that I just couldn't refuse," says Burke. "I was only 54, but they were telling me that I could retire quite comfortably right then and there. I took it."

Burke made his decision with the enthusiastic support of his five children and his wife, Barbara. Their marriage of forty years is the foundation of his life, he says. "We have so much respect for each other, and we make our marriage a priority," he explains.

Barbara Burke is a one-woman support team when her husband competes. He is also connected to a large, extended family of athletes. He trains with a bike club and swimming groups, and is also a member of the largest triathlon club in the world, with over 1,500 members (the St. Pete Mad Dog triathalon club, home-based in St. Petersburg, FL). Burke is Mad Dog #9 and the first member of the club to receive the Ralph G. Perry award proclaiming him Mad Dog of the Year 2000.

"These groups are wonderful," says Burke. "I mean, we had a new fellow come along recently who had a little trouble keeping up. He told us he had a kind of handicap. One leg was shorter than the other, and you could see that if you rode behind him on the bike. With our support, which included a little good-natured badgering, he really improved."

Helping others develop as athletes has become a passion for Burke. "I remember when my kids were in gymnastics and I'd go to the gym and watch their coach giving so much to them. Now it's like it's my turn. Things have come full circle, and I'm the one who has something to offer."

Besides helping new senior athletes train, Burke is involved in a project to create youth tri-athletes, and he is an in-demand public speaker. He doesn't always try to sell his audience on his particular sport. Instead, he tries to persuade the reluctant and fearful to take the risk of trying.

"A lot of people have had a bad experience and there was no one there to help them come back. Other people are convinced that they can't do anything athletic. Well, I tell them that everyone is good at something. They just have to remember the desire, determination, and energy they put into that activity and transfer it to something new. Find that passion and apply it and you will be successful."

CHARLES LASLEY, M.D.

Diet, Exercise, and Faith

A medical degree and a lifelong career in cardiac surgery have given Charles Lasley a rare perspective on health and longevity. "Modern man and woman hold much of their destiny in their own hands," he insists. "And the pathway to a long and vital life is clear."

"For most of time, mortality was caused by trauma," says Lasley. "People were killed by earthquakes, flood, starvation, freezing, saber-toothed tigers. After those were mainly overcome, the causes of death became infectious diseases. Now that we have dealt with most of those, the main cause is lifestyle. And 90 percent of the lifestyle problems people have are preventable."

"Prevention can be achieved in three relatively simple steps," adds Lasley. "First is abstaining from tobacco, drugs, alcohol, and caffeine which destroy your vital organs." Second is a high-fiber, low-fat diet. "Fat is your enemy," he says. Third is heart-friendly, aerobic exercise for one hour, three or four times per week.

If one man's example is proof, then Dr. Lasley's simple program works. At age 78 he is still an active surgeon who works in the operating room almost every day. He surfs, plays handball, runs and rides a bike to work and back — a total of twenty miles — almost every day.

"I do it because I enjoy it," he says. "But it's also a lifestyle that's supported by what I've learned. I've learned a great deal about the body and longevity, and it's given me some pretty strong opinions, feelings that have been acquired over a long period of time."

*   *   *

Charles Lasley first began learning about health and longevity while riding on horseback with his grandfather, a doctor who tended the sick in a Kentucky town of less than 500 on the border with Tennessee. "My grandfather practiced until age 88 and he was the epitome of the old-time country doctor," recalls Lasley. "He finally got a car, a Model T, after his horse fell off a bridge. I think he had three accidents the first month with that car because when he said, 'Whoa' and pulled back on the steering wheel, the thing didn't stop." He died at 98.

Even as a child Charles Lasley observed that bad habits, especially tobacco and alcohol, had a harmful effect on people. But for the most part, his lifestyle was typical for Americans in the South in the 1920s and '30s. "We ate a lot of pork and eggs and fried foods, and we salted everything so much it was like snow falling on our food." He was relatively healthy, except for ear infections which, in those pre-antibiotic days, contributed to a mild hearing loss that requires him to wear hearing aids today. "I also broke my leg in a baseball game that sort of turned into a football game," recalls Lasley. "But the truth is, I was very healthy and always have been."

Inspired by his grandfather, Charles Lasley went to medical school — Harvard — and after a series of residencies and a stint as an Army surgeon, settled into private practice as a cardiac surgeon. In the Army he had taken up running, mainly as a means to reach some wilderness areas where he wanted to hike. "But I did it to get somewhere, not because I enjoyed it."

It wasn't until he was settled in private practice that a fellow doctor, who was a long-distance runner, persuaded Lasley to just try pushing past the few miles he needed to cover to get from one place to another. "I finally decided to run further. It was seven miles that first time and it was great."

From that beginning, Lasley followed his own advice, building up his endurance. But sometimes circumstance would intervene and he would discover, almost by accident, that he was a stronger athlete than he knew. This occurred in a dramatic fashion the first time he entered a marathon.

"I had run ten miles before, so I figured I'd run half the marathon — about 13 miles — and then quit. Well, I got to the halfway point and stopped. Another fellow asked me if I was going to go on and I said 'No, my wife's going to pick me up here.' He told me, 'No she's not. There aren't any cars allowed out here. They closed the road.' I had no choice. I ran all the way back. So I did the complete marathon anyway."

*   *   *

Always an athlete, Lasley found it relatively easy to incorporate running and other sports into his daily routine, sometimes running to the hospital in the mornings, or to the gym at day's end. And he has kept it up all of his life. He has taken special interest in the medical aspects of fitness and reached some interesting conclusions. In the 1970s he was influenced by scientific work done on diet.

"I had been aware of a study of people who had lived in Holland during World War II when the Germans took away all their fats and milk products. Heart disease declined dramatically. And I also read about certain people in Africa who had almost no digestive problems, no diverticulitis, and no colon disease. They ate a diet that had a lot of fiber in it and they spent a lot of time walking with their flocks."

These reports, along with several popular diet books, convinced Lasley to drop his more typical American diet and embrace one that is built around fresh fruits and raw vegetables and grains.

Through personal experience, Lasley also learned to challenge assumptions about the body and aging. "In 1980 I injured my knee and went to an orthopedic man who said, `You've got to quit running. Maybe you'll still be able to ride a bike, but running is out.'" Lasley tried to follow the doctor's orders, but couldn't resist trying his knee again, once it felt healed. He discovered that if he used proper technique, and did not over-stress the knee, he could run without any discomfort.

"I think that 50 percent of people either over pronate or under pronate their foot and this can put abnormal weight loads on the knee," says Lasley. "A simple orthotic insert in the shoe can remedy the pronation and end the stress on the joint. That's why you'll find that elderly runners who are doing it properly have joints that are in better shape. You cannot wear that joint out if the load you're placing on it is correct."

Instead of reducing exercise and taking all stress off their joints, Lasley suggests that older people can benefit greatly from regular weight training done with proper technique to avoid injury. "You naturally lose muscle strength but you've got to fight it," he says. "An hour of torture lifting weights every once in a while can be very beneficial."

*　　*　　*

A devout Baptist, Charles Lasley had always believed in the importance of faith. But over time he has been convinced that spiritual and/or psychological well being also play a role in a person's long-term health and vitality.

"I'll give you an example from my practice," he volunteers. "I was scheduled to do surgery on this woman and she was waiting for her son, who's a minister, to show up. Well he wasn't there by the time we were ready so we went ahead, and the moment the anesthesiologist put her under she crashed. We had to stop and bring her back and cancel the surgery. The woman's son arrived shortly thereafter and prayed with me and his mother. Two days after," notes Lasley, "she breezed through the surgery."

As unscientific as this evidence may be, Lasley has seen this kind of thing happen often enough to embrace faith as one more powerful element in health. Add it to all the others, and anyone can maximize his or her chances for a vigorous old age that defies the negative stereotypes.

"People have to stop expecting to be old and run down and start expecting to be old and active," says Dr. Lasley. "The Bible says man can live to be 120 and I do think that's very possible today. That's what I expect; and I'll tell you something else, I'm going to try to live up to my own expectations."

LARRY YOST

From Adversity to Opportunity

Larry Yost was born in 1930, a year after the stock market crash and at the beginning of the Great Depression. His father was a forester who worked for the Civilian Conservation Corps, travelling the country to help establish parks and national forests. The family, Larry, his older brother Paul, and his mother traveled along with him.

"The travelling was a very broadening experience. It forced you to learn how to adapt. I did it by telling jokes," says Yost. "My brother did it by getting into fights."

Following these different paths, both Yost brothers achieved a great deal in their lives. The elder, Paul, rose through the ranks to eventually become commandant of the Coast Guard. Like his father, Larry Yost got a degree in forestry but he also added a second major, manufacturing. As a young man, he went into the furniture business and quickly became a mid-level manager.

"I literally poured everything I had into those jobs," he says, looking back on his career. "It's very labor intensive and the turn-over rate for employees was about 100 percent a year. That meant you were constantly training people, and constantly dealing with their mistakes and figuring how to correct them."

Yost had been a very avid athlete as a boy and a young man. "We were probably what you would call hyperactive," he says about himself and his brother. "But I also really liked the competition, and it was a good outlet for all that energy we needed to burn." In college — North Carolina State — Yost was a varsity swimmer for three years. It was there that he also met and married his wife, Jackie.

Once the responsibilities of work and family took hold, Larry Yost let go of his interest in athletics. More than a decade would pass until his brother challenged him to take it up again. "He was jogging at the time, and he asked me what kept me from doing it too. I said, 'Hey, I'm working every day from 7 AM to 5 PM and then I have to take care of my family. Just when do you think I should jog?' Then he said, 'What are you doing at 4 AM?'"

*   *   *

After that one teasing phone call, Larry Yost rose to his brother's challenge by rising a bit earlier every day. He began with a moderate jog of a mile or two, several times per week. Gradually he added more distance and picked up the pace. It was not long before he quit smoking to improve his breathing, and then he quit drinking alcohol.

"I realized that I couldn't smoke and drink at night and get up in the morning and run," he explains. "I developed friendships with other people who ran, and they didn't smoke or drink either, and that made it easier for me to stay away from it. Everything in my life was changed, gradually, and it all benefited my health."

As he reflects on this experience, Larry Yost realizes that to an important degree, life circumstances influence exercise routines. Most young adults starting families and careers cannot be expected to train in a serious way. But as circumstances change, and time pressures recede, opportunities for new athletic endeavors arise. Sometimes these opportunities come disguised as disasters.

*　　　*　　　*

"Losing my job was the best thing that ever happened to me. Of course, at the time I didn't realize it. At the time, I thought it was a terrible thing."

After more than twenty years in the furniture business, Larry Yost had a moment of truth on the floor of one of the factories he was supervising. As usual, he was under pressure from executives who tracked plant productivity on an hourly basis. The environment he worked in was noisy, and filled with both sawdust and tension. When a conflict arose with other managers, Yost was quite confident of the solution to a particular problem. They disagreed. An argument ensued, and he was dismissed.

"I got very depressed at the time," he recalls. "I was fifty years old and a lot of my identity was in that job. All of a sudden I felt like nobody needed me anymore."

Instead of casting about for something new in the furniture business, Yost decided to move to Florida. He bought a few buildings and became a landlord. He also opened a small home remodeling company, using the skills be had acquired as a woodworker. Even with this business, he had much more time to devote to the things in life that gave him pleasure: his relationships with his wife and children, and running.

"I got a new perspective on life, a more balanced view. I came to define myself more by who I was rather than what I was. Eventually I realized that getting fired was the best thing that could ever have happened to me. Now I recommend it. I think it should happen to everyone."

*   *   *

Yost and his wife, Jackie, live in Treasure Island, Florida, near one of the largest triathlon clubs in the world, the St. Petersburg Mad Dogs. Friends who were runners eventually introduced them to the sport, and they grew to love it. They train year-round, following a fairly strict schedule of biking, running, and swimming. To this they add weight training and the occasional round of golf.

"Now I feel like I have many different definitions of who I am," says Yost. "My triathlon friends know me as an athlete. Other people know me as a landlord. My wife knows me as a husband and her friend. We have a very close relationship. We train together, do everything together, really."

Together the Yosts have moderated their diets, and they approach their sport with a healthy respect for the risks as well as the rewards. "If you get injured at our age it can take you away from training for months while you heal. My approach now is to avoid injuries if at all possible. If I am hurting, I stop immediately before it gets worse. I listen to my body."

In Yost's many different definitions of himself, "Father" is high on the list; and he is proud that his attitudes about a well-rounded life and the value of exercise have been taken up by the next generation in his family. One of his adult daughters is training for marathons. The other is a player on two different soccer teams, and his son is an avid runner, though, because of his responsibilities at home and at work, not as active as his father.

"We're stride for stride when we run together," he says with a touch of pride. "Of course, I'm thirty years older than him."

IV

Iron Women

"The Iron Women" would be the last to say that their accomplishments are any more remarkable than those of their male counterparts in triathlons. They are right when they say that women can run, swim, and bike as fast and as far as men. But they are wrong when they insist there is nothing extra in their accomplishments. Today's senior women tri-athletes did grow up in a time when women were discouraged from participating in sports. In overcoming prejudice and pressures, they became pioneers as well as athletes.

JACKIE YOST

The Right Place, The Right People

Sometimes a person or a place can make all the difference in a person's life. When Jackie Yost, age 72, talks about the place where she lives — Treasure Island, Florida — she uses words like "perfect," and "sunny," and "paradise." Though she would have likely lived a very active life someplace else, Treasure Island makes it easy.

"Our house is right by the bay. This morning we took a bike ride for about twenty miles and had a little breakfast. On other days we will go for a swim, and maybe play some golf. It's a pretty perfect existence."

In many ways, the outdoor life that Jackie Yost enjoys today reflects another place — her childhood hometown in the Piedmont district of North Carolina. Though not exactly a tomboy, she recalls that she always preferred to be outdoors playing a game or embarking on some adventure. "I didn't like being pent up," she explains.

Organized sports didn't become part of Yost's life until eighth grade when the school she attended finally acquired a physical education teacher. Miss McBride was actually a teacher from the nearby state university, but she made a powerful impression on children who, until that point, had no instruction at all.

"We loved her because she taught us how to do new things," recalls Yost. "All of a sudden we were able to play all sorts of games, and we even had our own basketball team. Miss McBride was a wonderful person. She also invited her professors from the college over and they made quite an impression too."

One of those professors, Ellen Griffin, made such a strong impression that she inspired Yost to become a physical education teacher herself. She received her degree at the university where Griffin taught. It was there, too, that she acquired a life-long approach to sport that has made her a champion even today, at age 72.

*   *   *

"One of the most important things I learned at college is that you can learn a new sport and acquire new skills no matter what age you are. The key is to get the proper instruction and training."

Yost recalls that at college she discovered that she didn't know many of the swimming strokes that other students had mastered. But she was able to learn them, and practiced them in the pool and even in her bed, until she was proficient. "My whole freshman year I practiced, even in my mind, until I could do it," she explains. "And I was encouraged by my classmates. No one made any negative comments."

"Support is a second key ingredient when it comes to beginning a new sport or exercise program. Attitudes like optimism and confidence are shaped early in life," adds Yost; and hers were influenced directly by her parents, who raised their daughter to believe she could do almost anything. "My parents always had something positive to say about whatever I tried. And I could always see that my mother had athletic ability, although she didn't grow up in an era when she could express it. She was very agile. Very quick."

*   *   *

It was no accident that when it came time to marry, Jackie Yost found a man who understood how much she valued being physically active. From the very beginning they always played tennis and golf together. Even when her husband, Larry, was most deeply involved in his career, he still supported Jackie's efforts to improve in the sports. In retirement, they both took up triathlon racing. They bike, run, and swim together as members of the world's largest triathalon club, the St. Pete Mad Dogs. On some days, even that is not enough.

"I've had two holes-in-one in golf and the last one came after we had completed a triathlon in Naples, Florida," recalls Jackie Yost. "It was still pretty early in the afternoon so we decided to play 18 holes of golf. I was on a par-three hole, and I hit this 115-yard shot with a seven iron. Larry said, 'That ball is going to go in', and then it did. It was very exciting."

*   *   *

In golf, in triathlon and in other sports, Jackie Yost has been helped by expert teachers who offer both encouragement and the secrets of technique. She has always been very assertive in seeking out this kind of help. This willingness to learn new things and connect with new people has kept her active, she adds.

"Sometimes it seems like the older a person gets, the less willing they are to try something new," she observes. "You can see it with people as young as high school. If they haven't learned something, they feel ashamed and are very reluctant to try because they are afraid of embarrassing themselves."

"When you feel that way, it's important to have the strength of personality to try anyway, and it helps to find the right instructor or coach. Keep searching until you find someone you feel comfortable with. Then go take private lessons so you can learn the skills. Don't take lessons from someone who is not professionally qualified, and don't put up with someone who doesn't seem interested in really helping you. When you find someone who is right, stick with it. Do what they say."

"The same is true for other experts who promise help, including doctors," adds Yost. Recently, after suffering a crash on her bicycle, she was laid up with a broken clavicle. "I listened to what I was told and gave myself the proper time to recover. And I didn't let it stop me."

*   *   *

When she reflects on the factors that have contributed to a long, active life, Jackie Yost does not overlook genetics. "My mother lived until she was 90, and she was always active," she says. But she also recognizes the value of all the human relationships that have supported her along the way to a long, vigorous life. Those first physical-education teachers, her college instructors, her sports coaches, and her husband have all played key roles. Her children, Cindy, Joy, and Steve, have developed each in their own sport of running, swimming, soccer, and tennis. It is rewarding to have the love of sports passed on to another generation. They, too, are reaping the benefits of a healthy lifestyle. They, in turn, are passing it on to their families and others.

"Most of all, I'd say it was our marriage," she concludes. "We do things that we can share. And after we retired, we could enjoy them even more. I think of us the way we once thought of a little couple that lived near us when we were younger. They were in their eighties and we would see them out doing yard work, often clipping the same bush. That's the way we are now, clipping the same bush, and it's really nice."

Shirley Taylor

Meeting Challenges

For a long time, Shirley Taylor, age 67, was the swimmer who paddled behind all the others in a group of senior athletes that trained together in a little section of the Gulf of Mexico. When they reached a buoy and stopped, she was the one who had to say whether the group would swim on or quit for the day.

"I didn't know how to swim freestyle, and I was really not so happy about going into the Gulf," recalls Taylor. "I would say, 'Hey, there are things that are alive swimming out there. I'm scared.' The others in the group wouldn't let me stay scared though. They pushed me, and out I went."

The same kind of encouragement, and a desire to be a positive part of the group, motivated Taylor to say "One more buoy" as often as she could during their swims. Gradually her strokes improved as well as her stamina. And eventually she was not always the last person in the line of swimmers. "We tease and kid each other a lot. The camaraderie is wonderful," she explains. "And now I'm not always on the receiving end of all the jokes."

*　　　*　　　*

Though she has always been physically active, Taylor says that athletics were not central to her life growing up. "In the 1940s and 1950s there was not much available for girls. But I was a cheerleader through high school and into college at the University of Alabama."

Cheerleading was a way for a young woman who was raised "to be seen but not heard" to express herself. But it did not satisfy a strong drive to compete and excel, which she has felt for most of her life.

"I am a competitive person," explains Taylor. "But I didn't like the way that girls competed back then. It was mostly silly competition over boys and clothing. That just didn't make a lot of sense."

In fact, competing to beat another person was never Taylor's motivation. "It's more a matter of the challenge being important to me," she says. "If another person beats me, I congratulate them for doing their best, and I truly am happy for them. My goal is to get the satisfaction of knowing that I've been challenged and responded by doing the best I can myself."

Facing and then overcoming challenges has always been at the center of Taylor's life. She left the University of Alabama before finishing, but she never let go of her dream of earning a degree. At age 44 she went back to school in Ohio and succeeded. It was not easy being a returning adult student. But the diploma was key to advancing in her job as a technical librarian.

"I wanted to move up; I saw the challenge, and I went for it," she explains. "There was no reason why I shouldn't."

*   *   *

Shirley Taylor became a dedicated athlete when she took up running more than twenty years ago. She added other sports, like swimming, "because they were there" and because they presented a challenge. "I find it very rewarding to push myself past my previous performance. There's both a physical and a mental challenge in that and you get a tremendous sense of satisfaction when you succeed."

The health benefits of all this exercise include strength, stamina, and a level of cardio-vascular fitness that women twenty years younger than Taylor would envy. Taylor knows that she probably inherited a tendency toward longevity from her parents. Her mother lived to age 82 despite being a heavy smoker, and her father reached age 75. Aside from the occasional athletic injury she is in good health, and she supports this with a careful, but not too careful diet.

"I love my bread and other things like that, but I won't eat too much of anything," she says. "I have primarily a vegetable-based diet and I take plenty of vitamins, especially vitamin C and vitamin E."

*   *   *

Shirley Taylor says as a youngster, she never gave much thought to what her life might be like when she grew old. But she's pretty certain she never imagined having a large group of friends, participating in a great many sports, and finding new challenges and new achievements to enjoy.

"I was paddling in the Gulf of Mexico for only one reason—to become a triathlete. That was why I was forced to get into open water in the first place. I had managed to stay out of it until I was 63. I had to learn to ride a racing bike with my feet securely attached to the pedals. These were the challenges that scared me to death. The group support I received from those who were already accomplished triathletes got me passed the beginning stage. Now I have reached their level and have become a winner also," Shirley adds.

"I have to say," she adds with a bit of amazement in her voice, "I am living the happiest years of my life."

KATE KNIGHT-PERRY

Running With Love

The tale of Kate Knight-Perry's transformation from a tired, overweight and sedentary 40-year old into a long-distance runner and swimmer is, in many ways, a love story. Running brought the man she calls her "soul mate" into her life at a time when she had just about given up on ever finding true love.

"I first met Ralph literally in the middle of a road race in New York City," she recalls. Having worked much of her life in New York hospitals and New York visiting nurses, Kate returned to graduate school and became a professor of nursing. She had also just ended a relationship that had gone on for twenty years with the man in question unable to make a full commitment.

"By that time I was starting to think I would be alone," recalls Kate. "After all, the men who were my age were all interested in the young chicks, and if they had anything going for them, they could get one. But Ralph wasn't like that. He was interested in me as a person, and he had tremendous respect for me. From pretty much that moment on, it was Katie and Ralph together."

Together, Katie and Ralph Perry built a life around running, swimming, and biking in triathlons. This shared passion took them around the nation and the world to compete in events. Sport, and the man she had once feared would never come along, expanded Kate Knight-Perry's life beyond what she ever expected.

*   *   *

Kate Knight-Perry was born Katherine Knight on May 28, 1935, in Lake Placid, New York. In the third grade her family moved the few miles to Saranac Lake, and it was there that she would complete her public-school education. Always active and outgoing, in high school she was a champion on the school ski team. After attending a local junior college she went to nursing school at Cornell New York Hospital, fully expecting to go back to Saranac Lake when she was finished.

"Of course, you know what happens. You meet people and then when you graduate, a job comes up. I was offered a position at Cornell, and I took it. A few years later I went to work for the Visiting Nurses, and I loved that. I worked in Brooklyn and the South Bronx. I'd go up to one fifth-floor apartment and then go onto the roof to cross over to the next building. People would ask me if I wasn't afraid, and I never was. No one ever bothered us."

Almost before she knew it more then twenty years passed, and Kate Knight found herself feeling older and more tired than she believed she should. "I was forty and I had stopped all of the physical things I used to do, like tennis, because I had been working so hard," she explains. "I was heavy and I wasn't happy with myself at all."

Kate and a friend began to work themselves back into shape at Central Park. At first neither of them could run more than a block or so before slowing down to a walk. Their goal was to make one full lap around the reservoir — a distance of about a mile and a half — and they accomplished it in a couple of months. During this time, Kate felt the old competitive drive that she experienced as a young skier returning.

"When I started, I had no intention of competing in races; It was really just exercise. But the truth is, I hate training and I love racing. My first was a ten-kilometer race. Someone I knew just asked me if I was going to enter. I thought about it and figured, `Why not try?'"

Though she was hardly among the top finishers, that first race brought Kate back to the competitive arena and she felt almost like a young athlete again. She began running more seriously and racing in every event she could, including the New York Marathon. "The races provide a goal, a purpose," she says. "Without it, it would be very hard to train."

✳   ✳   ✳

Races were just one of the factors that motivated Kate Knight-Perry. Ralph turned out to be the other. From the moment their relationship began, Kate and Ralph exercised together, and he was always certain to keep her on her training regime. "If it was up to me and there was something that got in the way of going out on a certain day, I might let it stop me," she says with a laugh. "But Ralph was the coach, always keeping us on track. I liked that about him. He could be doing something and when the time for training came, set it aside and do what he was supposed to do. He made it a priority for both of us."

After they retired and settled in Florida, Katie and Ralph made running, biking, and swimming something like a new career. "It was our work," recalls Kate. And she did it well enough to win a shelf full of awards, including her age-group record for the 5-kilometer run. Serious sports were not all that Katie and Ralph did well. They delighted in the game of bocce, set up a court in their side yard, and promptly won a gold medal at a local Senior Games event.

This togetherness is the first of Kate Knight-Perry's recommendations for those who want to become senior athletes and gain the health, strength, and stamina she enjoys. Her second bit of advice has to do with setting the proper goals. "We are all only human," she says. "You don't have to be a superstar, just be your best."

*   *   *

Exercising together provided a purpose and an outlet for Ralph and Kate's lives. It gave them the opportunity to be their best at something. Though friends often teased them about their mutual obsession, they found in their sports both personal satisfaction and a large social circle in their activities.

"Eventually you meet other athletes and share a lot in common," she explains. "We were very active socially. And when you are with other athletes you don't have to explain why you need to go to sleep early, or want to eat certain things and not others."

Ralph and Kate gradually adjusted their diets to reduce

fats and increase carbohydrates. Between diet and exercise they both enjoyed remarkably good health. At age 65, Kate has never suffered from a serious illness, though she had coped with various exercise-related injuries. With a grandmother who lived to age 95, she is hoping that she has both genetics and lifestyle on her side.

Unfortunately, Ralph's health did not follow the same robust course at Kate's. In 1992 he was diagnosed with prostate cancer, which had already spread. He underwent surgery and battled the cancer for eight years. Through it all, he remained athletically active and optimistic. "He was holding his own, always saying he was about to go into remission," explains Kate. "Then a few months ago he took me to the airport for a trip. When I got back he had a stroke. He died soon after that."

*   *   *

For twenty years Kate Knight-Perry had leaned on her soul mate to help her become a top senior athlete. He was, of course, much more than a sports partner. He was the man who shared all of her passions, the man who truly loved her. He was her other half.

For a time after Ralph's death, Knight-Perry wondered

how she would endure his absence. "It's very hard waking up to an empty house," she says. It's also very hard to lace up her running shoes, knowing that the only footsteps she will hear on the path will be hers.

But the coaching that Ralph gave her, and the love as well, remain, she says. And she refuses to let go of the rewarding life she built with him. Recently she set another goal for herself. She is training to compete in a triathlon in Hawaii. She knows she will make it to the race, and finish it in Ralph's honor. "After all," she explains, "it will be run on his birthday, and he'll be there in my heart."

V

Queens of the Diamond

Millions of American women hold fond and exciting memories of playing softball or baseball as girls. Most let go of the game and in adulthood have nothing but memories of the sport. In the early 1990s a group of women in Northern California recaptured the game for themselves. The first was Barbara Racine, who began playing with other teams. But it wasn't long before her enthusiasm turned into a team that now fields at least a dozen real athletes.

BARBARA RACINE

Always a Ball Player

Barbara Racine has been a ball player, a real ball player, from the day she was big enough to swing a bat. She played on champion fast-pitch softball teams as a girl in her home town of Marquette, Michigan, and continued playing during a stint in the Air Force — where she picked up the nickname Raisin — and throughout her career as a civilian employee of the Navy.

"I played fast-pitch until I was fifty years old, and then got into slow-pitch," says Racine. "But when I was about fifty-two, I went to the local Senior Games and found out that they didn't have softball. I got the gold in the discus and the shot-put right away. But what I really wanted was to play softball."

By 1989 Racine had won gold medals in the State of California Senior Games and found herself going to St. Louis for the National Games. In St. Louis she met a group of fifty-five+ Colorado women, who were going to the Games to play softball.

"I say, 'hey, I'd love to play!'" she recalls. The rules allowed for teams to field a couple of out-of-state players, and the Colorado women welcomed Racine to join them. In 1993 Racine, still without a home-town team, connected with a group from her home state of Michigan. This time she won a gold medal and returned to California determined to find a team she could practice and play with regularly, or create her own. She wound up creating her own team, finding players by word of mouth, and simply introducing herself to older women she saw at ballparks.

That first Northern-California team was an eclectic group of seasoned softball players, newcomers, and gifted women athletes who had never before taken the game seriously. Among them was Joanie Weston, famous in the Bay Area as a roller-derby skater, and Joanne DiMaggio, 'Joltin' Joe's' niece. Two local women's track legends, Irene Obera and Cherrie Sherrard also played. That first team — named the Silver Streaks — was one of just two that competed in the State Games, so both qualified to attend the Nationals Senior Games.

*   *   *

In 1994 Barbara Racine created the Silver Streaks – a team for those age 55+, and then the first team in Northern California. Today, there are seven women's teams in Northern California, one for 60+, the Silver Streaks, and six teams for 50+.

The Silver Streaks continue today with 12 of its original members, and the quality of play has improved greatly. Now when California teams go up against powerhouses from the East and Midwest, where women's softball is more popular, they can compete. "Last year we came in sixth out of twelve teams," explains Racine. "We lost to Canada in a game we really could have won."

When she talks about the game, Racine's voice grows lighter, happier. "It feels so good when you get a hit or make a really good play," she explains. "I always played third base because I was a good fielder and I could make that long throw over to first base." Ask if she has had any health problems, and she responds like an athlete, describing problems with strained muscles and a surgery to repair an injured hand. When she finishes talking about herself, she goes on to discuss her teammates.

"Our pitcher is out with an injury; she's had rotator cuff surgery on her shoulder but she's coming back. She's seventy. And then there's our first baseman; she fell in the beauty parlor and hurt her shoulder."

Suddenly Racine realizes that she may have skipped

over something important in her answer. "Oh, you're asking if I've had any health problems related to aging," she says with a laugh. "No, I have to say I've been pretty healthy my whole life. I think it has something to do with being active."

Softball requires that Racine stay active in many different ways. She organizes teams and games, coaches, and coordinates practices. All these jobs keep her in close contact with a vast network of women. "Sometimes it can be difficult to round up players. We'll have a practice and a lot of people can't make it. Then, at the Games, you might deal with male umpires who are disrespectful or act like they just aren't interested."

Despite these obstacles, Racine can see that the benefits outweigh the costs. Her team is made up of women of all races and sexual preferences who come to cherish their differences and their friendships. Several players on her team live alone, on minimal pensions. The team offers them companionship and regular social outings with no real financial cost. "We play to win, but we also play for the camaraderie. We don't want to be on the porch in a rocker, knitting. We want to play."

For most of her life Racine has noticed that this simple desire to play ball was shared by many other women who were either too shy to get involved, or simply couldn't allow themselves the pleasure of devoting themselves to a game. Now, after a lifetime as a pioneer in the game, she sees this attitude changing.

"The number of younger women who are playing just grows and grows," she says. "There are teams all over the place for women under forty, and many more than there used to be for older women." The quality of play has improved, too. "A lot of women are into weight training. They go to the gym. We didn't have these things when I started, but you can see how it helps so many women stay stronger. We women are getting stronger and stronger."

*   *   *

Softball has given Barbara Racine much more than an outlet for her athletic abilities and competitive spirit. It has been the setting for many of the important moments of her life, and it is a well spring of happy memories.

"The team I played on when I was young, in Marquette, included a couple of players who actually went on to play professional baseball," she says with pride. "I played softball from the moment the snow melted in spring until it came back again in the fall."

"Now, it's exciting to see so many women playing, so many teams where they can enjoy the game as much as I do. Once, when I was watching a couple of teams play, one of the women came over to me and said, 'You know Barbara, you're like the mother of us all. You are behind all of this.' That made me feel pretty darn glad to have been a ball player and glad that I never gave it up."

Barbara reminds us that healthy aging is contagious. She says, "In August 2000 in Hayward, California, I met Dot Richardson of the USA (Gold) Softball Team. With her love of the game I told her she could play into her sixties and seventies due to the growing number of senior women's teams. The dream continues..."

CHERRIE SHERRARD

Twice an Olympian

Like most mothers, Cherrie Sherrard seems to be more interested in talking about her children than about herself. Her two sons, Roy and Mike, are very accomplished athletes, she says. Mike was even a professional football player. He was with four teams, including his hometown San Francisco 49ers.

"A lot of their interest in sports came from my husband," she explains. Robert Sherrard, raised in the bay area of Houston, Texas, who died in 1997 at age 65, played basketball all over the world on behalf of the United States Navy.

If you allowed her to stop talking, Cherrie Sherrard might leave you with the impression that all the athletes in her family are male. But question her a little, and Sherrard, who is 62 years old, will confess that she's an athlete too. She's a key member of the Silver Streaks senior women's softball team. But that sport is not her main interest. "I've done a little running," she says.

A little running, indeed. Beginning in the late 1950's Cherrie (pronounced Cherry) Sherrard struck fear in the hearts of women sprinters and hurdlers for the better part of a decade. In meets where she battled against the legendary Wilma Rudolph and other greats, Sherrard was an extremely tough competitor. She was a member of the U.S. Olympic Team that went to Tokyo in 1964, and won a gold medal at the 1967 Pan American games. She accomplished these two feats after having her first child.

"I might have done more if I hadn't started so late," says Sherrard, who didn't begin running until she was almost sixteen years old. "Of course, I also might have done better if I had trained a little harder," she adds, laughing at herself. "I didn't train as hard as I could, but I always had fun. I always enjoyed myself."

*　　　*　　　*

Though slowed considerably by the passage of time, Cherrie Sherrard can recall the feeling of her body flying down the track and bounding over the hurdles. She felt sheer joy in the power and grace of her own movement. But when she considers everything she has gained from staying active in sport, she tends to focus on the people she has known and the places she has seen.

"I think a lot of what happens to you in life, especially

when you are young, depends on the crowd that's around you. I made a lot of good friends in track. I mean, the truth is, you are only competing for about fifteen seconds at a time. The rest of the time you spend socializing. And athletes tend to be very positive people. They all have goals, something they are working to achieve; and they really are, for the most part, supportive of each other."

As an athlete himself, Robert Sherrard was completely accepting of his young wife's decision to return to the track after she became a mother. "There was no question that he was there for me," she recalls. "He was proud to see me do well."

Sherrard ran competitively until she was almost thirty years old. She had an operation on her leg to remove a benign growth, and for a period of about five years seemed to have disappeared from track.

"Then I started to get back into it," she recalls. "I got involved in some events for older runners, Masters events (35 and up), and when I was fifty I also ran (50 and up) and continue to do so. I won most of the time. And you know what? I enjoyed winning just as much then as I did when I was young. It was still very satisfying."

* * *

Although winning feels the same at any age, Cherrie Sherrard says that other aspects of athletics actually become even more satisfying when you are a senior. "You still have the challenge, and the travel and experiences you have mean more to you," she explains.

"When I went to the Tokyo Olympics in '64, I don't think I really appreciated it all fully. I was young. And when you are in the middle of something like that it's very hard to grasp. Now when I go someplace to compete with seniors I notice everything, enjoy everything, more than I did before."

Sherrard says that one of the most valuable lessons of her Olympic experience came after her return. Simply being an Olympic athlete brought her many requests for public appearances where she would be asked to speak. "This made me very nervous, so nervous that if it was a banquet or something, I couldn't eat," she explains. "I kept thinking, 'I am the same person I always was. Going to the Olympics didn't make me a great public speaker.' Then I realized that all I had to offer was the real me. If I mess up, I mess up. So what? After I accepted that I could only be myself, it got much better."

❊   ❊   ❊

At 62, injuries and age have pushed Cherrie Sherrard off the track, but she still throws discus and the shot-put at the Senior Olympics. She walks two miles per day, bowls in a league, and plays outfield for the Silver Streaks. "I can still move, especially compared with some of the other people on the team," she says. But just as she learned to accept herself as a nervous public speaker, Cherrie Sherrard has learned to accept herself as an athlete, who has become a senior, but stays in the game.

"You've got to accept the changes in your body and move on," she advises. "I take my turn at bat when they call my name and if our team's not that good, so what? We have fun. That's the right goal for me now that I'm over the hill. I have fun."

In pursuit of her new sports goal — having fun — Cherrie has recently turned to a game that she finds more frustrating and, in some ways, more challenging than any she had ever tried: golf. "It's embarrassing when you are an athlete to take a swing at that ball and not even hit it," she says. "But I'm having fun and that's what matters."

IRENE OBERA

Performance Not Excuses

When Irene Obera was a little girl her father used to say, "Make performance, not excuses." That sage bit of advice has been her watchword ever since.

Reno, as her friends call her, has done so much in her profession as an educator and in the field of sports that it's difficult to know where to begin in listing her accomplishments. But it's not impossible.

Irene, a sprinter, was elected to the first Hall of Fame for the U.S. Amateur Track and Field Masters Athletes. She has twice been selected Master Athlete of the Year. And she has won a medal in every event in all the World Championships in which she has ever competed.

In her professional life Irene went from being a physical-education instructor to department chairperson, to counselor, and ultimately, to being the first female principal of Berkeley (California) Continuation High School, a position in which she won a Merit Award.

"People don't need to put limits on themselves," says Irene. "I feel like a complete person when I'm competing. I love testing myself. It keeps me young."

*   *   *

Born in 1933, Irene Obera was one of seven children who were raised by loving parents in San Bernardino, California. "We were all spoiled," she recalls. "So I really never went without anything. But maybe since there were seven of us, that made me more competitive."

Irene's father encouraged his children to participate in sports. It was, according to Irene, a reaction to the disappointment he suffered in his own youth when he made the Philippines All-Star Baseball Team and his parents refused to allow him to travel to Manila.

Irene's first foray into sports came in the ninth grade at a school-sponsored sports day. "I didn't know a thing about softball, but I got up and hit a home run." A left-hander, Irene has been hitting home runs, literally and figuratively, ever since.

After graduating from Chico State College with a degree in Physical Education, Irene taught at the California Youth Authority, which operates juvenile detention centers. Soon she moved on to the Berkeley School District as a teacher and ultimately as a principal.

"I spent ten years as a principal and then I felt the need for a change," said Irene. She decided to return to the classroom again, and rounded out her professional career by teaching both physical education and computers.

"I retired in '94, and since then I'm having a lot of fun," she said.

*   *   *

For Irene Obera fun includes playing on the Oakland Silver Streaks Women's Slow-Pitch Softball team, competing in Masters' track, playing tennis, bowling, field hockey, doing weight training, and nurturing a beginning interest in golf. Many of these activities are with the Senior Games. Tennis is her newest new passion. She and her friends play on three different teams each week.

"If we like a sport, we just go and jump in. I always start for fun and then I want to be #1," she said.

The desire to be the very best at whatever she tries has driven Irene throughout her sports career. Just last year in England, for instance, she set world records in the 100 and 200-meter events at the World Association of Veteran Athletes (WAVA). Her time was 14.29 in the

100-meter. Her running has taken her to events in Sweden, Germany, New Zealand, Australia, and Puerto Rico, to name but a few places.

Irene's role models are drawn from the field of sports. She admires Monica Seles and Martina Navratilova. And she reveres women's' track legend, Wilma Rudolph, whom she ran against many times.

"Wilma was a real champion," explains Irene. "I used to say to her, 'I'm always pushing you to world records.'"

Today Irene considers Cherrie Sherrard, a personal friend since college days and a teammate on the Silver Streaks, as something of a mentor, although Cherrie is five years younger. It was Cherrie who first got Irene interested in playing Senior slo-pitch softball, and it was Cherrie who encouraged her during her first track meets.

"We're good friends and arch rivals," said Irene. "Cherrie and I compete constantly. She once told me, 'If you'd compete against others as hard as you do against me, you'd really be bad!'"

* * *

Although she is devoted to sport and competition, Obera approaches the rest of her life with similar enthusiasm. In what few spare hours are left in her hectic schedule she works as a police volunteer with the handicapped-enforcement parking patrol and the radar team as well as anywhere else the Fremont Police Department needs a volunteer.

At the age of 67, Irene, a single woman, is the picture of health. She eats a lot of vegetables, fruit, and fish, but indulges herself each day with a bowl of ice cream. With her heavy schedule of sports activities it's hardly necessary that she do any other type of formal exercise to keep in shape. Indeed, just about everything she does contributes to her physical health.

"I love making a race out of everything. I like to do everything fast. But I don't have to always be doing it alone. I like team sports, too, like the Silver Streaks. I consider myself a team player."

LUCILLE LIGON

The "Energizer Bunny"

In this day and age when friendships seem to come and go with the speed of e-mail, it's not only refreshing but almost unheard of to find three women who see each other constantly and have remained the best of friends for more than forty years.

The bond between Lucille Ligon, Cherrie Sherrard, and Irene Obera was formed back in 1958, when they all attended Chico State College in California. While the three women's personalities obviously blended well, it is their mutual love of sports and the thrill of competition that give an extra dimension to their closeness. They are each other's greatest fans in the stands, and each other's toughest rivals on the field.

"My sports activities are usually against Cherrie and Irene and I'm always third," says Lucille. "I'm particularly in Cherrie's shadow. But she is my best friend. She taught me all I know about sports. She is our ringleader."

Cherrie, Reno (as Irene is called), and Lucille do not compete against each other all the time. They are also teammates on the Oakland Silver Streaks of the Senior Women's Slow-Pitch Softball League. And when they are at the top of their game, they can strike fear in the hearts of senior-women's softball teams throughout the state of California.

*　　　*　　　*

Lucille Ligon was born in Picayune, Mississippi in 1938. She and her twin brother and two sisters moved around the country with their mom and dad. Her father was in shipbuilding, and his career took the family from Mississippi to Oregon, and eventually to California.

The family was not greatly interested in sports, although Lucille's brother played some sports in college. Lucille became involved in sports in college; and in her case, it led to a decision to major in physical education.

But her career in Phys Ed was short lived. After a year of teaching, Lucille opted to become the first woman police officer in the Vallejo, California, Police Department.

"At first I was the only woman in the police department; later I was one of three women," she recalls. "And, yes, some of the men did give me a hard time."

Despite this, Lucille stayed with the police force for 19 years.

She remembers with particular fondness her work with drug-prevention programs, which involved going to area schools and speaking with the students.

It wasn't until the early '90s, when Lucille was 53-years-old, that Cherrie recruited her to join the Silver Streaks.

By that time Lucille had retired and had more time for sports. She agreed to play shortstop, and when needed, the outfield. She rounds out her participation in the Senior Games by also taking part in the shot-put, discus, long jump and the 100-meter dash.

*   *   *

Lucille's immersion in the Senior Games — seizing opportunities to compete in several events — reflects her active approach to all things. When she retired, she immediately became a volunteer health-care worker, using the skills she acquired caring for her disabled mother for the last four years of the older woman's life.

Volunteering led to a second career. Today, Lucille works as a medical assistant with the Kaiser-

Permanente Medical Group. The full-time position curtails her ability to travel widely and limits her participation in sports to the weekends. But she has found time to compete in the National Senior Games in Texas, Arizona, and Florida and has high hopes for attending the International Games. She picked up a second-place medal in track and field at Orlando.

Fortunately, Ligon has been blessed with the health to keep on competing. She has never suffered from a major health problem, although she did once tear her Achilles heel during a game of basketball. And like many of her peers, Lucille has never had to diet or follow any formal exercise program.

"I probably should begin to think about such things as diets," says Lucille. "It gets harder every year."

From the outside no one could guess that Lucille feels any strain. "My friends think I'm like the Energizer Bunny, I just keep going," says Lucille. "I try to convince friends who aren't involved in sports to join us. I tell them we need more people. I tell them about the 94-year-old golfer who participated in the Games in Arizona. They talk about it but they never really do it."

*　　　*　　　*

On a recent Saturday afternoon, Lucille, Reno, and Cherrie went together to bowl competitively in the Senior Games and later went out to dinner to celebrate Cherrie's birthday. In the day's competition Irene had come away with a silver medal in her doubles match. Lucille was not so fortunate.

"I was trying to bowl, but after today, I probably won't go that route," says Lucille, whose performance apparently left something to be desired.

But the rest of the day was a rousing success. The three long-time, best friends were like college kids at the birthday dinner, laughing and having a great time, as they always do when they get together.

JANET W. PARKER

Never Too Old to Play

Nearly 30 years ago the very young coach of a woman's fast-pitch softball team in Chico, California, told Janet Parker she was "too old" to play. Janet was in her forties at the time.

Today, at the age of 70, Janet Parker plays on three teams, one of them the Oakland Silver Streaks of the Senior Women's Slow-Pitch Softball League. She also coaches softball, runs in 100 and 200-meter races, coordinates a coed volleyball event, pitches horseshoes, and on many an evening, dances up a storm. She can't quite recall what happened to that coach who proclaimed her "too old" to play.

*   *   *

The first time Janet ever threw a softball she was a kid playing in a potato field in rural Massachusetts. She didn't take up the sport seriously until many years later following a stint in the US Army, the births of her four children, and a move to California.

The couple married in March 1950. Janet was assigned

to Fort Riley, Kansas, while her husband returned to Fort Churchill, Canada, to finish a tour of duty.

"It was kind of weird. I was 19, a real homebody, and I had never traveled. I thought I'd like to play professional softball but had no contacts to get my foot in the door, so I joined the Army. I did get to play softball on the WAC [Women's Army Corps] team at Fort Riley, Kansas for a short time but ended up having emergency surgery and had to drop off the team," said Janet.

Janet was proud to be named "Outstanding Recruit" in basic training, and was allowed to choose one of the Army's special-skills schools. She chose to attend Army Finance School in St. Louis, and it was there that she met her husband-to-be.

In March 1951 Janet became pregnant, and Outstanding Recruit or no, the U.S. Army threw her out. That was the military's official policy for handling pregnancy a half-century ago.

*   *   *

With Janet out of the Army, the family relocated to California when Janet's husband switched his military affiliation to the Air Force. Time passed, the four children grew, and eventually Janet found more and more time for her beloved softball.

Since her husband's death in 1996, Janet has found that sports and dancing occupy most of her time. She's traveled to Florida, Arizona, and Texas with the Senior Games and has her sights set on the Nationals in Louisiana in 2001. Her sports include softball, running, and horseshoes. When she's not competing on the sports field, Janet cuts a mean figure on the dance floor.... it's a family trait.

"My parents were beautiful ballroom dancers. We used to go to the Grange and dance there," she recalls. Her father, a businessman, also played some softball; and her mother was a swimmer, as well as the mother of seven children.

Through the Senior Games, Janet has found a couple of good dancing partners. Unfortunately, following a dance at the Senior Olympics in San Antonio in 1995, she slipped on a wet patch of lawn and injured herself. That injury recurred in the spring of 2000 and resulted in Janet having to undergo rotator-cuff surgery. (Not a good thing for a pitcher.) Fortunately, her recovery was quick, owing to her excellent physical condition.

"I was operated on by the same surgeon who works with the San Francisco '49ers," she adds, proudly. Janet's conscientious and upbeat attitude toward all that she values spilled over into her rehabilitation, which she took very seriously. "I even wore my sling and went dancing. But I think just wanting to get back out there helped as well," she said.

A month after the surgery she began to practice pitching. Within weeks she felt strong enough to start preparing for the California State Senior Games. Before long, she was also back to pitching horseshoes. "Lob pitching and pitching horseshoes are kind of the same motion," she explains.

When she returned for her one-month check up, the surgeon was "real happy" with her progress, by the second-month's check up "he was grinning ear to ear."

The doctor could grin, as well, over Janet's medical history. Told a decade ago that her cholesterol level was "border line," Janet immediately cut down on fats in her diet, although she still manages to work ice cream into her "required regimen." At 5'6" and 137 pounds, this 70-year old is just about ideal on the height and weight charts.

*   *   *

The Silver Streaks practice in Oakland. Janet lives in Durham, some 150 miles away. No problem. She practices regularly near her home and makes the trip to Oakland one or more times a month to work out with the team.

While many of her friends are people she meets through her participation in sports, others are not. "Those other friends are kind of shocked about all that I do, and sometimes I think some of them feel left out. But I've chosen to do the things I wanted to do, and my lifestyle makes it possible to do them," Janet said.

Asked if there are any role models in her life, Janet immediately named Cherrie Sherrard, a key member of the Silver Streaks and a runner in the Tokyo Olympics in '64.

"Cherrie Sherrard is something else again," said Janet. "She's won a Gold Medal at the Pan Am Games, she does discus and shot-put, but she's also a really neat person, a nice person."

VI.

The Green Table Gang

Small things can make a difference. In the case of four very different men in the Chicago suburb of Bolingbrook the small thing is a green table-tennis table. Every week these men give their all in competition. During their games they discover the limits of their abilities and the joy of the game. Afterwards they enjoy friendships that would never have blossomed without the green table.

Simplicio Copiaco

Spirit of the Survivor

At age 79, Simplicio Copiaco is the eldest of the Green Table Gang of seniors that plays table tennis twice per week at the Levy Senior Center in Bolingbrook, Illinois. He is also a regular in the pick-up softball games that are played every few days during warm weather. Tall, with black hair that is turning silver, he runs the bases fast enough to cause his hat to fly off his head. And he can still get his glove down low to scoop up a grounder at second base.

Slender and flexible, Copi, as everyone calls him, is blessed with a body that has stayed healthy and has allowed him to win ten medals — from bronze to gold — in a variety of Senior Games events. But like many of the more active, older athletes in the games, he believes that he has thrived because of his spirit more than his body.

"I have noticed that there is a spirit of the survivors, and a spirit of those who give up," he says. "I definitely have the spirit of the survivor."

*　　*　　*

Few people endure the kind of test Simplicio Copiaco underwent to discover that he has the survivor spirit. Born in a small town in the Philippines, he was the son of a businessman who ran a fleet of horse-drawn taxis. One of six children, he had three brothers and two sisters. Through high school he was an avid athlete, playing every sport available to him, from basketball to badminton.

After attending public school and then his second year at the University of the Philippines, Copiaco was drafted to fight under General Douglas MacArthur against the Japanese in World War II. His division was among the first reserves sent to meet a Japanese invasion. Three quarters of the group was killed within days of its deployment, and Copiaco joined the rest of the army that mounted a three-month desperation defense of the Bataan Peninsula. Their defeat and surrender was followed by the infamous Bataan Death March, which saw thousands die as they were forced to cover hundreds of miles on foot in the jungle heat.

"I saw a lot of people who just lost the will to live," recalls Copiaco. "They got malaria, dysentery, cholera, or they simply laid down and died. I knew that I didn't want my life to end there like that, with no dignity. I was determined to live, and it turned out that three children were the ones who actually saved me."

The first child was standing by the side of the path watching Copiaco and a group of stragglers stagger ahead. The boy was carrying a bucket of water and Copi, literally dying of thirst, lurched out of line, seized the bucket, and began to drink. He took in at least a quart, and kept drinking even as a guard beat him.

The second child appeared just as Copi was hatching an escape plan. He had spotted some civilian clothing in a heap beside a bridge and crept off to switch some of them for his uniform. On the other side of the bridge he saw a group of civilians whom a guard was directing away from the POWs. This time the little boy was crying and lost. He allowed Copi to take his hand, posing as his father, and lead him across the bridge. There he was ordered to join the civilians, and he melted into the crowd.

The third child savior was an infant who began bawling on the tiny ferryboat that Copi had hoped would carry him across the bay from the peninsula to Manila, where he could disappear in the city. A Japanese patrol boat stopped the ferry. Sailors searched it and the commanding officer, convinced that some of the passengers were escaping soldiers, ordered that everyone on board be shot.

"They told us to say our prayers and aimed machines guns at us when this baby started crying," recalls Copiaco. "The officer said he could not shoot the baby, so he insisted that the mother give him the baby. He promised to take care of the baby. But the mother refused. We all sat huddled in that boat, praying, for a long time. In the water we could see the bodies of other people and soldiers who had been killed. Then, all of a sudden, he just let us go. Just like that. It was like a miracle."

*　　　*　　　*

The miracle of his survival made Simplicio Copiaco believe in the power of prayer and the strength of the human will. He has relied on both of them to guide his life. "But prayer is my number one weapon when I have problems," he adds. "I use it every day."

After a career in the Army, Copiaco was a physical education instructor and then a school principal. In 1983 he retired and moved to the United States, where his daughter, one of his seven children, lives with her American husband.

"When you have survived something like I have survived, then you go through the rest of your life without any fear," he explains. "I am always very grateful for the gift that is my life. I have faith that God has a plan for me, and that includes the afterlife."

Sport, especially the Senior Games, became a focus in Copi's life in the 1990s, when he started competing. "I like the competition, and I especially like winning," he smiles. But it is not the only activity that he uses to keep his body, mind, and spirit strong.

"I really like to be useful and to work," he says. "I drive my wife to work every day and my grandchildren to school. I enjoy having responsibilities like that and keeping them. But the thing that really helps my attitude is working hard in my garden. I grow vegetables and flowers. It is really wonderful to work out there and see things grow."

Copiaco credits his diet — a traditional Filipino diet that emphasizes rice, vegetables and fish with his good health, and his marriage of nearly fifty years to his wife, Henrietta, with his happiness. "I think having someone who knows you completely is very important; and my wife, she knows me completely, and she still loves me. I love her in every way," he adds with a wink. "Now it's only every two weeks or so, but that's okay with me."

Prayer, a survivor's strength, exercise, diet, and a marriage that is still sparked by passion are Copiaco's full recipe for a good life after seventy. "And the best thing is if you have these things, you don't feel 70," he adds. "I run the bases as well as I did when I was fifty or sixty. I don't feel a day older."

STAN LISZKA

Mr. Fun

It had been a good day for Stan Liszka. He was undefeated in his regular, Monday morning table-tennis round-robin. Even though it was afternoon, and the competition was hours old, he still felt a glow.

At age 68, Stan Liszka is six years into retirement, and six years into Senior Games table tennis. He began as a good but unsophisticated player. "In the beginning the best player at the senior center here, Ken Palmer, beat me all the time," he recalls. But he replaced his hard-faced, old-fashioned paddle with a spongy, high-tech model. And he studied his opponents' moves. Now, on any given day, he has a good chance of winning every match he plays.

"Winning the competition is great, but the workout we get is actually pretty strenuous. You work up a sweat, sharpen your reflexes. And maybe the most important thing of all is the camaraderie and fun."

        ＊   ＊   ＊

Camaraderie and fun are important to Liszka. They practically flowed from the taps at the neighborhood tavern in Buffalo that his father owned and operated throughout his childhood. The first and only male child, with three older sisters, Stan Liszka's arrival on this earth was greeted with cheers and toasts. As soon as he was walking and talking, he was visiting his father at work and soaking up the affection of the regulars. This experience established early some of the habits and personality traits that would last a lifetime.

"I guess I'm a little bit different than the other guys who play in the Monday game," says Liszka as he moves behind the elaborate bar he has built in his family room. Behind him, neon signs, mugs, mirrors, and beer-brand mementos fill the wall. Overhead, Christmas tree lights twinkle all year long. And near the doorway waits a plastic, mounted trout that will sing for you at the touch of a button.

"I'm the type of guy who will have a beer, and maybe eat some of the things that they say are bad for you. A lot of guys absolutely refuse to do those things. But it hasn't hurt me." Liszka may have genetics on his side. His father lived to 92 and his two sisters are 78 and 76 and still active.

"The fact is, I am as healthy as I have always been." Muscular and clear-eyed, Liszka appears much younger than his age. "I don't have heart disease, or diabetes, or arthritis, or prostate problems," he explains. "What I do have is a very positive attitude. I am very flexible, and I believe I can do anything."

*   *   *

Stan Liszka's first serious lessons in attitude were handed out by the priests who ran the Catholic boarding school in Erie, Pennsylvania, where he was captain of the baseball, basketball, and football teams. Liszka was sent to Erie for his junior year after he began having attendance problems at another school.

"In school I hadn't been into sports in the same way, and I hadn't really focused on what I was supposed to do," he recalls. "It was very hard to adjust to living away from home. And there was one priest in particular who wasn't reluctant to give anyone a beating. But I straightened out pretty fast. I really got into sports, and it saved me."

After boarding school came a brief stint at college. Then, at the height of the Korean War, Liszka decided to follow in his father's footsteps. Without telling anyone, he enlisted in the Marine Corps. His father's reaction was not what he expected.

"My Dad just said, 'Oh, my God,'" recalls Liszka. "He was real worried for me. He told me to keep my chin up and my mouth shut and just get through it."

"It" was basic training at Parris Island, which began with Liszka obeying the order to strip off his civilian clothes and kneeling, naked, to have his head shorn. Life got much tougher after that. "They literally made a couple of guys just crack up," says Liszka. "But I got through it. I don't know how, but I did."

Basic training and three years of duty gave Stan Liszka a sense of confidence and fearlessness. He couldn't believe that life held any greater challenges than those posed by the drill instructors at Parris Island. For the most part, he was right. But like everyone, he did endure some deeply personal crises. The worst came in 1985 when his marriage of twenty-seven years, which had produced two sons and two daughters, ended in divorce. Though he is now happily remarried, "I still remember how painful that time was. I don't deny that it took a long time to get over."

*   *   *

As he talks now, it's hard to imagine this buoyant man ever exhibiting much pain or sadness. He says that even during the rough times, he remained physically active and essentially upbeat. This resilience was key to his success in the insurance business, where he worked for thirty-eight years. "I loved meeting the people, sitting at their kitchen tables," he adds. "I never got tired of it."

The word "tired" doesn't seem to be in his vocabulary. Besides table tennis, Liszka is an avid golfer. He plays regularly with his second wife, Kristine, one of his grown daughters, and his two grown sons. He also works as a ranger at a local club, delivering water and otherwise making the game go smoothly for whoever is on the course. Whatever he does, he makes it a point to have fun.

"Quite simply, my secret is to have as much fun as possible," he advises. "Our team from the senior center travels around the area playing other groups and we beat them all. It's really exciting. The sport gives me something to look forward to all the time. As long as I'm on my own two feet, I'm going to play."

EDUARDO SANABRIA

Sport as Therapy

At first the grassy patch behind the house on Charleston Street looks like any other suburban backyard: patio, barbecue grill, table and chairs. It's quiet, sunny, a nice place to fall asleep to the music of the birds.

But then you notice that on one side of the yard a board has been staked into the ground and a wheelbarrow-load of sand has been dumped a few feet beyond. Just past the sand, a yellow rope has been stretched across the turf. This is no ordinary backyard. It is Eduardo Sanabria's training ground. The board and the sand help him measure his progress in the standing jump. The rope is his target whenever he hurls the shot-put.

There's more out front, where a basketball hoop has been installed for foul-shot practice. And inside, down-stairs, a bench and free-weights stand ready for work-outs. All of it — the sand pit, the hoop, the weights — is for a man who almost gave up on life, but now burns with a competitive desire that keeps him working out five or six days per week.

At age 59, Sanabria has transformed his home to support his commitment to sport and the annual Illinois Senior Games, where he competes in half-a-dozen events. Stocky, broad shouldered, and strong, Sanabria is primed for the competition. But the Games and his training represent much more. They have been at the core of a rehabilitation program that has brought him out of blindness and back to the richness of life. He explains all this on a summer day after his workout is over.

*   *   *

"The accident happened in 1993. I was a chemical technician. I don't know if something from the bench or my gloves contaminated things." While testing a chemical reaction, Sanabria noticed his goggles fogging up. To get in air to clear his goggles, he removed his gloves and moved his goggles forward. Accidentally, he touched his eyes with his chemically-contaminated finger. He was instantly blinded.

At first physicians held little hope, but when eye specialists saw that pieces of retina remained, they suggested a series of operations to restore partial sight in one eye. Thus would begin an odyssey that brought Sanabria to the brink of despair and back.

"For the first time in my life I couldn't really do anything," he recalls. "I couldn't drive. I couldn't move around. I couldn't work. I couldn't even watch television. I was very angry a lot of the time. Without my wife, Anna, I don't know what would have happened to me."

Anna and Eduardo had been married 35 years when the accident happened. They had met in their native El Salvador, when Eduardo, the son of a pharmacist, was enrolled in medical school. He dropped out when they married and then immigrated to the United States in 1970. "Something told me that trouble was coming and to get out of my country and find opportunity here," says Sanabria. In fact, a long civil war did come to El Salvador, and in leaving, he escaped both military service and the danger faced by civilians.

In the U.S., Eduardo went to college and became a chemist in order to provide for his family. Anna, who is five years younger than her husband, worked too. Along the way, the couple had found a home in the Chicago suburbs and had four children. "Everything was real beautiful," he recalls, "until the crisis."

The surgeries performed on Eduardo's eyes came in rapid succession. For the better part of two years he was either in the hospital or recovering. During much of his recovery he was required to limit his activities. Just bending over or rolling in his sleep could damage the delicate work done by his surgeons.

By 1998, the operations brought blurred, partial vision and he faced the prospect of rebuilding his life. "My wife finally told me that I seemed quite angry a lot of the time. I had to do something." He began by a visit to the local senior center, where he was among the youngest. There he heard the rhythm of table tennis and was invited to play. The men who asked him to join them didn't know that this newcomer could barely see.

"I could not drive. I could not read. I could just barely see their faces," explains Sanabria. "But for some reason, I could see that little ball."

Tentatively at first, Sanabria managed to handle the basics of the game: serving and returning serve. As weeks and months passed, he was able to extend rallies, and then win a few points. And something else improved, along with his game: his sight.

"I can't explain it, maybe it's just because the game made me focus and exercise my eye, but it got much better," he says. "I realized it was like therapy. And I loved doing it."

* * *

Not long after his first visit to the senior center, Sanabria learned that his table-tennis friends were preparing for the Senior Games, which are held every year in Springfield, Illinois. They looked at his strong body, considered both the state of his table-tennis game and his youth, and suggested he try track and field.

"They told me about the shot-put event, the discus, basketball, and jumping. These were things that I had done in high school, and I had been pretty good at them. I thought about getting back to those sports, and then about what the doctors had said about exercising. There was a little conflict."

The conflict was resolved during a consultation with his doctors. They continued to object to heavy weight lifting, because straining could put pressure on his eyes. But they recognized the physical and psychological benefits Eduardo had reaped through table tennis and agreed that he could try the other events.

"They had a list of the records set at the Senior Games and I used my magnifying glass to study them. I set my goal — to break those records — and began my training."

Though he has been consistent in his training, Eduardo does not follow a rigid schedule. He throws the shot-put and discus every other day to allow his muscles time to heal from the stress. He works on his jumping on the other days, and will shoot baskets and run sprints in the street whenever the mood strikes him.

The workouts make Sanabria feel stronger, more energetic and calmer. He combines them with a diet that is heavy with vegetables and light on meats and fats. He doesn't smoke. He takes multi-vitamins. And he saves the occasional beer for celebrations or hot afternoons when he's finished mowing his lawn.

All of it — the practice and the diet — is directed at the competition that he faces each year. The results have been inspiring. Consider, for example, his first try at the standing jump.

"I had been practicing and my best was something like seven feet two inches. But the people I saw in Springfield were very, very good," he recalls. "I saw one person jump over eight feet three inches. In my first two tries, my best was seven two. Then I thought to myself, 'I'm going to let myself take flight.' That was when I jumped seven feet, nine and a half inches. I didn't win, but I did my very best. That's what competition does for you."

In two visits to the State Games Sanabria has collected a total of eleven medals. He has also acquired a large group of friends, many of whom are older, that by their example show him a bright and lovely future.

"When I began participating in sports again, it gave me better health," he sums up. "Now I say that it gave me a better life. I am learning every day from my own experiences and from the experiences of my new friends. Through sport, I didn't get my eyesight all back, but I did get back some of my life."

Summary

Thinking About Tomorrow

As we have seen, "the face of aging" is changing. This is happening in our lifetime because three forces have come together with a multiplying effect.

First, science is succeeding. There will be more discoveries in the next 10 years than in the past 100.

Second, nature is forgiving. Our bodies can tolerate a certain degree of unhealthy behavior as long as permanent organ damage has not occurred. Eliminating smoking, expanding exercise, adopting a healthy diet, lowering stress, participating in regular cancer screening, establishing a long-term relationship with your doctor, and staying on your medicines all have a healing effect. And of course, the earlier you begin, the better.

Third, attitudes towards mature seniors are changing, making it possible to not only live longer, but also happier, and with greater independence.

Timing makes all the difference. We know that only a handful of diseases are responsible for turning healthy vital seniors into frail, dependent adults. These include arthritis, high blood pressure, heart disease, diabetes, Alzheimer's disease, stroke, and depression.

A healthy diet, no smoking, moderate exercise, and strong family and social networks decrease the likelihood of these diseases. But even with good prevention, a certain number of people with a strong predisposition or family history will face one or more of these disorders as a challenge. The key for these individuals is early diagnosis and proper treatment. In most every case, if the problem is identified early, before there is damage to the body, the disease can be controlled and held in check indefinitely. If you control it, it won't control you.

What we've seen from our senior athletes is that they were religious about seeing doctors early and having preventive screening in their forties. In contrast most Americans wait until their fifties or sixties. Our athletes checked their hearts with cardiograms and stress tests, prevented cancer with colonoscopys, mammograms, and blood-screening tests, and picked up diabetes, hypertension, and early heart disease at office visits before the age of fifty. They stayed healthy because they took action early.

Staying healthy and vital also means that our society benefits in many different ways. A fully-functioning mature senior is important to our economy. Seventy percent of the financial resources of our society are in the hands of those over fifty. As consumers, seniors purchase forty percent of all new cars, seventy percent of all prescription drugs, and eighty percent of all luxury travel. And their presence in the workforce has kept our economy healthy and expanding. By 2010 it is estimated that twenty-one percent of all workers will be over sixty five.

In addition to labor, healthy seniors are an enormous creative resource, providing both wisdom and honest critique. Montaigne said, "I speak the truth not so much as I would, but as much as I dare, and I dare a little more as I grow older." In an age of tremendous explosive change in technology, science, and communications it is vitally important that we benefit from the wise, direct, and honest critique of fully-engaged seniors.

As our stories have demonstrated, not only do seniors benefit from their good health, but so do their families. Many of our athletes are the senior member of four or even five-generation families. By staying healthy, vital, and independent, they spared the generations below the responsibility of caring for them. This in turn, left the second and third generations more time and energy to devote to the first generation, our nation's future — the children. The truth is that staying healthy as a mature senior is good for the individual, good for your family, and good for our country.

The goal of early diagnosis and treatment is to extend both the quantity and quality of our healthy years. And since none of us live forever, there will come a time when care will be required from others. When that time comes, none of us should be too proud to ask for help. We should realize that this final phase of life has a redemptive feature to it.

As others care for us, we form them. Through us they will be appreciated, challenged, and educated. Through us they will learn of dignity, simplicity, and humility. Through us they will be forced to consider if their lives are balanced, if their time has been well spent. These, too, are the contributions of mature seniors. We live our lives as teachers by placing our lives, when the time comes, in others' hands.

In the meantime, we can all benefit from the advice of a group of senior celebrities who we joined in an appearance on Larry King Live.

Art Linkletter – Age 81
"Keep your hand on the tiller of your own life for as long as you can."

Bob Dole – Age 78
"The most important thing is getting into the doctor's office early."

Barbara Eden – Age 64
"It's wonderful to be able to just be yourself and not have to wear shorts, and a bikini, and worry about your navel."

Ed McMahon – Age 77
"I like to be old. I just don't want to get old.
I'm proud I got to here. I'm not done yet."

Jane Russell – Age 79
"I ride a bike, and I swim, and I keep busy, and I sleep. I love to sleep. I love to sleep."

Willard Scott – Age 67
"I think one of the great things is to hang around younger people. That keeps you younger. And the other thing is to be happy. Have a nice attitude about life."

✳   ✳   ✳

The "new face of aging" is about adopting that "nice attitude about life." In being introduced to this wonderful collection of human beings we hope you come away inspired to do two things.

The first is to take good care of yourself. You are uniquely valued and may underestimate the good you do.

The second is to make the most of every day of your life. That life has touched many others in a most remarkable way. Reach out, stand up, smile, touch, and embrace. The "new face of aging" is your face—a mirror of your special skills, personality, life experiences, treasured memories, and beliefs. Let it shine and reflect on others.

Additional Resources

www.healthyliving.com